THE
WORLD OF THE
LURCHER

Author's Notes

It is important for me, a mere scribe, to ensure that readers do not confuse me with my namesake, perhaps the most experienced lurcher breeder of all time. I produce words; he produces pups. His black merle and beardie-blooded lurchers are renowned throughout the sporting world and his lurcher photographs have graced many publications. Any references to Hancock-lurchers are to his produce and not connected to me in any way at all.

The word 'lurcher' describes a function, not a breed of dog, rather as the word 'gundog' describes the various breeds of dog working to the gun. Historically, the lurcher was the 'stealer' or 'the thievishe dog', utilised by the humbler hunter, often hunting unlawfully. Like gundogs, lurchers vary in size, coat, head structure and precise function, with Deerhound, Smithfield and Bedlington lurchers being quite distinct from the Bull, Whippet and Bearded Collie types. Dogs portrayed in antique art, displaying the sighthound phenotype, are usually described as belonging to the nearest similar contemporary breed, rather than as lurchers, despite hunters of the past placing performance well ahead of purity of breeding. Today, any mongrel with the sighthound silhouette can attract the loosely applied title of 'lurcher' but the automatic association with unlawful hunting has thankfully lapsed.

OPPOSITE:

Breed historians are quick to seize upon historic references to 'greyhounds' and 'deerhounds' as breed mentions. But in ancient times, before pure breeding became established for its own sake, every smooth-haired sighthound would be termed a Greyhound and every hound used on deer termed a Deerhound. In Russia the word borzoi referred to a swift dog rather than a distinct breed. By type and often by function such dogs were in fact lurchers.

THE WORLD OF THE LURCHER

Their blood, their breeding and their function

David Hancock

Quiller

Previous books by the author:

Dogs as Companions – 1981
Old Working Dogs – 1984 (reprinted 1998)
The Heritage of the Dog – 1990
The Bullmastiff – A Breeder's Guide Volume 1 – 1996
The Bullmastiff – A Breeder's Guide Volume 2 – 1997
Old Farm Dogs – 1990
The Mastiffs – The Big Game Hunters – 2000
The Bullmastiff – A Breeder's Guide – 2006 (one volume hardback edition)

First published in the UK in 2010
by Quiller, an imprint of Quiller Publishing Ltd

British Library Cataloguing-in-Publication Data
A catalogue record for this book
is available from the British Library

ISBN 978 1 84689 078 9

Printed in China

Quiller
An imprint of Quiller Publishing Ltd
Wykey House, Wykey, Shrewsbury, SY4 1JA
Tel: 01939 261616 Fax: 01939 261606
E-mail: info@quillerbooks.com
Website: www.countrybooksdirect.com

DEDICATION

This book is dedicated to the lowly lurcherman, the humbler hunter. His hunting desires have long been thwarted, over several centuries, by intolerant landowners, misguided magistrates and over-zealous law-makers. Persistently persecuted and perennially lacking rights or privileges, the humbler hunter and his hunting dog may lack a written heritage, but, despite every obstacle, have preserved and passed on hunting skills which one day may well be valued once again.

Striving to feed a hungry family is surely a noble aim.

Poachers

It is not correct to think of poachers as peasants hunting illegally; much of the latter, in Tudor times especially, was conducted by the gentry themselves. In his well-researched book *Hunters and Poachers*, Clarendon Press 1993, Roger Manning tells us that in Sussex between 1500 and 1640, 15% of all poachers were peers and gentry, despite being only 5% of the total population. He writes that 'Poaching was becoming a national pastime in Tudor and early Stuart England. Poachers came from a wide variety of backgrounds. Those from the landed and propertied classes – peers, gentlemen, merchants, and yeomanry – organised themselves into poaching fraternities.'

Poachers and Keepers

'The greatest deer-stealers make the best park-keepers.' M P Tilley, *A Collection of the Proverbs of England*, 1950.

Scale of Poaching

Historically poaching was conducted on a large scale. The poaching gang operating in the New Forest in the 1620s was over 50 strong. In Yorkshire in 1640, a poaching gang of around 40 killed over 70 deer in Wortley Park. The infamous Russell gang of 1619 ranged over four counties, carrying away 327 red and fallow deer, 1,000 hare, 1,400 rabbits, 5,000 pheasants and 1,000 partridges.

THE 'THIEVISHE' DOG
The word lurcher was originally used to describe a 'thievishe' person and then a 'thievishe' dog. Lurchers have also been called 'stealers', 'look-dogs' (especially in East Anglia) and 'night-curs', from poachers using them mainly at night.
(Norfolk Museum Service (NRLM Gressenhall))

COURSING NEEDS

'All coursing men pay particular attention to depth of chest, quality of back and loins, and still more to the hindquarters – i.e. the rump, the first and second thighs as well as the hock joints and pasterns. It is almost impossible to be too insistent regarding highly developed muscles and broad loins, where so much action is brought into play when a Greyhound is running and twisting after the hare.'

Frank Townend Barton MRCVS, *Our Dogs*, Jarrolds, 1938

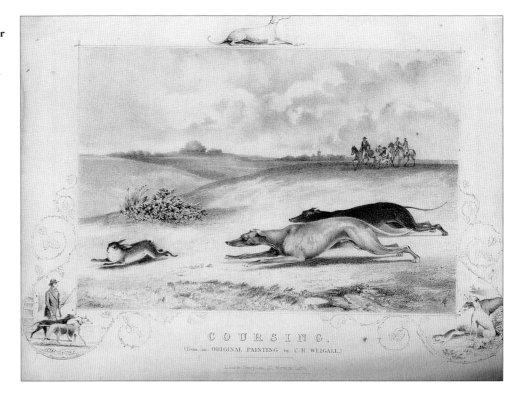

COURSING.
(from an ORIGINAL PAINTING by C. H. WEIGALL.)

London Henry Lea, 22, Warwick Lane.

SIGHTHOUND PHENOTYPE

In the United States, the sighthound breeds appear to be losing breed-type in the pursuit of a 'sighthound' general pheno-type, arising from the seeking of 'TRAD' (tremendous reach and drive). This is resulting in over-long vertical necks, set at a strange angle to the shoulders, shallow croups, and over-angulation in the stifle. In time, in the exhibition world there, the functional sighthound will disappear, as the desire for a stat-uesque exhibit imposes a false stance-led type.

Persian.   English Greyhound.   Deerhound.
Italian.   Siberian Wolfhound.

THE GREYHOUND FAMILY.

CONTENTS

The most numerous type of dog in Britain; rooted in working class breeders, long lacking in nobler patronage. Remarkable popularity of cross-bred sporting dogs, purity of breeding never revered by hunters. Effectiveness the only real test, the proven value of mixed blood.

The origin and purpose of the lurcher, the hunting dog of the peasant and the poacher, now favoured too by the well-heeled, not just the farm labourer, with shows proliferating from sheer interest. The lurcher as a functional dog, from a blend of breeds, its anatomy allowing hunting prowess. The desire to hunt more important than physique. Essentials of breeding as set out by experts. Importance of ingredient/contributing breeds. Selection of breeding stock the key. Understanding genetics important. Heredity passed on randomly not mathematically. Dominant and recessive traits. Perils of too close breeding. Overuse of certain sires not wise.

The value of Collie blood: cleverness and obedience, sagacity ahead of speed, eagerness to work prized. The value of Deerhound blood: size, strength and coat, vital to match anatomy with terrain. The input of Bedlington Terrier blood: terrier persistence and waterproof coat, selection of breeding material the key. Use of bull lurchers is historic and specific; mastiff ancestry, bandogge role, hunting mastiff background. The coarsely bred catch-dogs of the boar-hunt; boar-lurchers, complementary use with scenthounds, impact of Alauntes, role of different Alauntes, mastiff and bandogge functions. Big Greyhounds used as wolf-dogs, Irish and Russian breeds survive, medieval value proven.

Hunting by speed, development of the sighthounds, deficiencies of show ring hounds, sighthound phenotype rooted in function. Impact of the Greyhound, remarkable pace from anatomical make-up. Gazehounds different from sighthounds; Greyhounds replicated abroad: Galgo, Chart Polski and Magyar Agar, supreme canine athletes. Desert sighthound, the Saluki: great stamina, long-distance sprinter, good feet, difficult to train, widespread use in North Africa and Middle East. The miners' Greyhound: the Whippet, amazing sprinters, tenacity from terrier blood, importance of heart and liver size and lung room, crucial role of sound shoulders; must be conserved as a sporting dog. The loss of the English Deerhound – the 'strong Greyhound', discarded once deer hunting with scent hounds was preferred.

The show ring type. The need for schooling, handling and pre-show training, vital importance of condition. Lurchers must never be bred for show-stance ahead of pot-filling prowess, must not become canine film-stars. Rabbits have to be controlled; absence of specialist rabbit hound. Universal need for rabbit-culling; US style different. Difficult prey making a good hare-dog look stupid. Problems of using terriers with lurchers, value of Beagle blood. Scope for bobbery packs, using hounds and terriers together in packs, new role for the Airedale. Shows can never help selection of breeding material, best regarded as social gathering. The vital importance of sound shoulders. The crucial role of the loin.

The desert sighthounds, often out-crossed, different types of Saluki: the Middle Eastern dog, Sloughi is the Arab dog, Azawakh is the African. Varying types of Indian lurchers. South African hunting dogs, remarkably robust, surviving harsh climate and testing terrain. Mediterranean littoral abounding with lurchers: Portugal, Spanish Islands, Malta and Gozo, Sicily and Crete, all bat-eared sighthounds of Tesem type. Are field trial regulations for lurchers needed here? Enormous scope of steppes for sighthound work, well-known Borzoi, unknown Chortaj, Tasy, Taigon and Circassian Greyhound. The American Staghound, used on wolf, coyote and hare. All used as lurchers on wide variety of quarry.

Eternal role, certainty of catching game with hounds against likely maiming with guns. Loss of instinctive canine skills, threat of feral pig, value of lamping dogs. Remarkable survival of the lurcher down many centuries. Vital need to keep the blood alive.

Lurcher of Reinagle *c*1800.

Lurcher of Cecil Aldin *c*1900.

INTRODUCTION

'...to the mind of many, the most intelligent of all (sighthounds, D H) is the Lurcher, rather blown upon as to his reputation through his association with the Romany, but a creature of singular parts. He, I suppose, approximates to the hunting dog employed by our remote ancestors in that he can still be relied on to catch, kill and deliver one's dinner wherever game is to be found.'

Brian Vesey-Fitzgerald *The Book of the Dog*, Nicholson & Watson, 1948

The most popular breed of dog in the United Kingdom is the Labrador Retriever, with over 45,000 registrations with the Kennel Club each year. But it is estimated that around 50,000 lurchers are newly born each year but registered with no body. There are around 100 lurcher shows a year, some featuring lure-chasing and high-jumping. But the lurcher has no breed standard and no breed clubs as such. The Association of Lurcher Clubs (ALC) was formed in 1995, with the idea of uniting the various small lurcher and coursing clubs in a joint purpose. It offers support to lurcher owners and helps fight for the restoration of hunting and coursing with lurchers. The ALC is a full voting member of the Council of Hunting Associations. In conjunction with the National Working Terrier Federation, the ALC aims to promote and support all kinds of hunting with lurchers and terriers, working to a code of good practice and with the permission and goodwill of landowners, farmers and the police. Such an organisation deserves the support of lurchermen across the home countries; a united voice can achieve so much more than individual ones, which are so often used only when difficulties arise. No need has arisen for health schemes in lurchers. Lurcher owners and breeders don't seek regulation, the whole background for this type of dog is rooted in villager-breeders, poacher-owners and performance-related prowess rather than pedigree-dog posing.

In just one recent issue of a country sports newspaper the following dogs were on offer: Beagle X Harrier hounds, Beagle Dachshund X Beagle Jack Russell, Saluki X Greyhound pups, Springer X Foxhound pups and what was termed 'the ultimate lurcher' pups: dam – Ridgeback X Greyhound, sire – Best Belgian Malinois in the country. These hybrid products were in addition to the usual lurcher advertisements, normally a mix of Whippet, Bedlington Terrier, Greyhound and Collie blood. All these hybrid products are the direct result of sportsmen seeking better hunting dogs, a timeless activity. Purebred dog breeding only came about when the breeding stock merited such a step; it was conducted by informed breeders desiring stability of proven lines not the blind pursuit of purity for purity's sake.

The lurcher and terrier men have of course long ignored the sanctity of the pedigree and pursued effectiveness i.e. performance in the field. Shooting men by and large seem to copy their show ring counterparts, despite the unprecedented occurrences of inheritable diseases in the gundog breeds, the loss of 'type' in so many Labradors, English Springers looking more like Cockers, the loss of the true colour in Golden Retrievers and yellow Labradors and the deterioration in field performance of the minor breeds. How long ago it seems that very competent cross-bred retrievers competed at field trials!

In their classic *Genetics and the Social Behavior of the Dog* (University of Chicago Press, 1965), Scott and Fuller report: '...breed intercrosses might be used to produce superior working animals... it should be realised that a breed is a population of individuals

Historic Lurchers.

Sighthounds – Show Greyhound and Irish Wolfhound.

showing a limited but still important degree of genetic variability. If selection is confined to one narrowly defined type, the result will almost inevitably be the accidental selection of various undesirable characteristics.' They went on to state that breed standards should also cover health, behaviour, vigour, and fertility, as well as stipulating body form. They suggested that obedience and field trials were a valuable step in influencing the selection of breeding stock. My reservation about that would be based on a worry that the dogs which excel at responding to human instructions are not always those able to think for themselves.

In his *Dog Breeding* of 1994 (Crowood), Frank Jackson writes: 'The vigour of recently recognised breeds provides evidence of the value of the wise use of cross-breeding.' He points out that these crosses make it easier for the breeds to retain genetic health after they have been recognised, as recognition immediately puts a severe restriction on the size of the breeding base. One advantage of the recent blending of Parson Russell Terriers with Jack Russell Terriers is that the breeding population in the combined breed gives far greater flexibility in developing future breeding lines. The white working Lakeland Terrier, as Frank Jackson reminds us, did much to infuse new blood, and a better anatomy, to the emergent Jack Russell. This use of outside blood to improve the breed is not possible now that KC recognition has been obtained. This may suit a registry but does not make for the best practice in breeding sound dogs.

There is no such thing as a pure-bred lurcher.

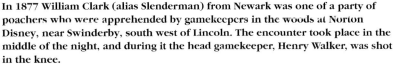

'The outcast of dogdom, not recognised as a breed by any kennel club or society, and frowned upon by dog-lovers and sportsmen. But the true lurcher is a true breed all the same, breeding true to type, and very carefully bred by certain Gypsy families... A dog of great speed, hardiness, and wisdom, which can be trained to do all manner of almost incredible feats.'

Brian Vesey-Fitzgerald, *The Book of the Dog*, Nicholson & Watson, 1948

'The Lurcher is by no means the ugly brute he is sometimes described to be. True, they vary greatly, and the name more properly describes the peculiar duties of the dog, and his manner of performing them, than distinctiveness of type.'

Hugh Dalziel, *British Dogs*, Upcott Gill, 1888

'All along the moorland road a caravan there comes
Where the piping curlew whistles and the brown snipe drums;
   And a long lean dog
   At a sling jig-jog,
A poacher to his eyelids, as all the lurcher clan,
Follows silent as a shadow, and clever as a man.'

Patrick Chalmers, *The New Anubis*, 1936

In 1877 William Clark (alias Slenderman) from Newark was one of a party of poachers who were apprehended by gamekeepers in the woods at Norton Disney, near Swinderby, south west of Lincoln. The encounter took place in the middle of the night, and during it the head gamekeeper, Henry Walker, was shot in the knee.

He later died of the injury and Clark, accused of firing the shot, was convicted of murder and hanged, the last man to suffer the death penalty at the Castle.

His dog, a lurcher, had accompanied him everywhere, even on drinking sessions at the *Strugglers Inn*, at the junction of Westgate and Union Road, just outside the north–west corner of the Castle. After its master's capture the dog was left at the public house, and is said to have pined away. It was stuffed, and for a number of years was on display in the bar.

The dog was presented to the Castle some years ago, and after being refurbished by a local taxidermist and a new case made, was put on display in the Castle. It was later put into storage until March 2007 when after being once again inspected and cleaned by a taxidermist it was placed on general display by the Friends of Lincoln Castle.

A great deal depends on selecting the greyhound bitches from strong and plucky strains. There are what we may call short-distance as well as long-distance greyhounds. The latter are much preferred for our purpose.

From *The Confessions of a Poacher* by J Connell (1901)

Well, now I will tell you how to train the Dogs, as for netten rabbitts and hars one must have a dog. The best breed of dogs are a cross between the Smithfield cattle dog and the greyhound, as you get the greyhound speed and the Smithfield sence. The pup must have a broad head across the eyes, as that is were he keep his brains, deep chest, sturdy legs and plenty of coat.

From *I Walked by Night – Being the Life and History of the King of the Norfolk Poachers* edited by L Rider Haggard, Nicholson & Watson, 1935

The Russian Greyhound destroyed wildboar and wolves.

CHAPTER 1

THE HUNTER'S ULTIMATE PERFORMANCE DOG

Looking at Lurchers

Judging a Lurcher

Selecting a Lurcher

Genetics and Hybrids

Gamekeeper with his night-dog on the look-out for poachers.

Ben, a lurcher by Lucy Kemp-Welch.
Courtesy The Tryon Gallery

ANCIENT TYPE
As a type of dog, the lurcher was recognised over 200 years ago. In the Linnaean catalogue of dogs, published in 1792, the lurcher is identified as 'canis laniarius', one of 35 recognised types, with the Greyhound listed as 'canis cursorius'. In this catalogue the lurcher was described as having a narrow body, long legs and being covered in short thick-set hair. Interestingly, the rough lurcher was listed separately, as 'canis laniarius aprinus', with the boar lurcher also named, as 'canis laniarius fuillus'. (Charwynne Dog Feature)

Night-dog seizes poacher and warns off Lurcher: *The Poacher* by Richard Ansdell (1835)

LOOKING AT LURCHERS

'In the stern-sheets a brace of the real Fen longtails curl up in the straw, their snaky heads and wet black noses nuzzling confidentially at one's calves. They may be 'look-dogs', but I will lay half a sovereign that they can smell the three great mutton sandwiches stuffed hastily in the right-hand pocket of the old shooting jacket.'

James Wentworth Day, *The Dog in Sport*, Harrap, 1938

For a thousand years in Britain, the humbler hunters have had their own special dog, with pride in its performance rather than its purity of breeding, yet purpose-bred in the pursuit of hunting excellence just as shrewdly as any Foxhound or gundog. Forever associated with gypsies, poachers and country characters, the lowly lurcher has survived the campaigns of rural police forces, watchful gamekeepers and wary landowners, and to this day, still keeps the pot filled for many a working class household. Yet nowadays the lurcher fancier is classless; blazers and cavalry twill feature as much at lurcher shows as moleskin and mufflers. The phenomenal rise in lurcher shows in the last forty years demonstrates the awareness of interest in these extraordinary hunting dogs of mixed parentage. But it has also brought, at times, a tendency to breed a type that will win 'on the flags' rather than a 'chase, catch and kill' champion.

But what is a lurcher? If you look around at a lurcher show it is soon apparent that the event would be better labelled 'any variety, sporting dog', for the height, weight, coat and colour are essentially anything but uniform. For a lurcher must be a cross-bred dog – fast enough to take all legal quarry, crafty enough not to get detected when used by the poacher, and able to withstand the cold and the wet, as well as the odd encounter with barbed wire. Purists might say it should really be a Collie X Greyhound to be truly a lurcher; but Deerhound, Whippet, Saluki, Bedlington Terrier and Beardie

blood have all been used over the years to instil dash, greater stamina or a more protective coat.

It is common to find the less diligent researchers linking the 'tumbler', quaintly described by a number of 16th century writers, with the lurcher. Correspondents contributing to country sports magazines on the subject of lurchers often sign themselves 'Tumbler'. But the tumbler was the decoy dog, a very different animal. Dr Caius, for all his learning, knew little about dogs, and yet has over the years become much quoted as some form of authority. But even he mentioned the 'Thevishe Dog or Stealer, that is a poaching dog'. His lengthy and extraordinary description of the 'tumbler' is in effect an exaggerated account of the antics of the decoy dog. I know of no lurcher which hunts by 'dissembling friendship and pretending favour' as he describes.

The decoy dog of England has been lost but the blood lives on in the Nova Scotia Duck Tolling Retriever and the Kooikerhondje of Holland. The first named luring the inquisitive ducks to within range of the hunters' rifles; the second enticing them along ever-narrowing little waterways until they are netted. We have lost the 'ginger 'coy dog' of East Anglia, referred to by such rural affairs writers as James Wentworth Day. But whereas the red decoy dog is perpetuated in distinct breeds, the lurcher was and ever shall be a nondescript dog. As 'Stonehenge' described them a century and a half ago: 'A poacher possessing such an animal seldom keeps him long, every keeper being on the look out, and putting a charge of shot into him on the first opportunity... the poacher does not often attempt to rear the dog which would suit him best, but contents himself with one which will not so much attract the notice of those who watch him.'

A farm labourer's dog is not so easily researched as that of the squire, but 'Stonehenge' has managed to convey the vital ordinariness, the essential anonymity and the fundamental disregard for type in what has long been a cross-bred purely functional hound, used for illegal hunting. A minority prize the Smithfield blood from the old drovers' dogs and there are usually the more bizarre crosses, such as Airedale X Whippet or Bearded Collie X Dobermann Pinscher. The normal combination however is that of sighthound with herding dog, with more recently, Kelpie and Malinois blood utilised.

Judges at Kennel Club dog shows have scoffed at the whole business of even attempting to judge such a wide variation of type in one lurcher ring, but, of course, that is exactly what they do when judging 'Best-in-Show' when all the winners in each breed competition come together to compete with one another. Lurcher show judges are not conformist anyway, having included such diverse characters as Moses Aaron-Smith, a gamekeeper from Derbyshire, born in a gypsy waggon of pure Romany stock, Ted Walsh, a retired Army Colonel and expert on coursing, and Martin Knoweldon, a commercial artist specialising in the depiction of sighthounds in full stride. The lurcher world, despite the establishment of the National Lurcher Racing Club, with regional branches, has never needed an infrastructure, a tight organisational body.

Overseas, a number of breed-types act as lurchers: the Banjara Greyhound, the Cretan Hound, the Portuguese Podengo and the Ibizan Hound. But our lurchers can possess a wide range of skills, being not just fast running dogs, but able to use ground and air scent and track quarry as well as course it. The lurcher of Britain can be a combination of coursing Greyhound, retriever, tracker, pointer and watchdog. It would be more correct to describe the word lurcher itself as indicating a role, rather than a distinct type of dog. For it doesn't matter if a lurcher is 20 or 26 inches at the shoulder, rough-coated or smooth, black and tan or buckskin, prick-eared or drop-eared, provided it is biddable and can run. Uniformity of conformation matters little, but composition matters a great deal: good feet with strong toes, plenty of lung room, a flexible back, well-angled shoulders and immense power from the hindquarters are essential. The lurcher has to look like a hunting dog.

'No dog in Britain ever drew more fire than the lurcher, not even the sheep-worrier. The gamekeeper hero of a novel by G Christopher Davies, Peter Penniless, lies in wait for some poachers who are about to gate-net a field, having stopped the meuses. As the poachers approach, accompanied by their lurcher dog, which has been trained to drive the hares directly towards the gates..., Peter asks his employer what he should do if the dog scents them. The employer, elderly gamekeeper Quadling, replies, 'Shoot it. That's why I brought my gun. The men may be too quick for us, but I thought we might have a shot at the dog'.'

Carson Ritchie, *The British Dog*, Robert Hale, 1981

'...the Black Act of 1723 restored the death penalty for the stealing of deer... a host of other activities connected with deer stealing – the possession of traps, trespassing at night, or trespassing in the company of a lurcher – were made capital offences by the same act...'

Emma Griffin, *Blood Sport*, Yale University Press, 2007

POT FILLER

'For centuries, the lurcher has been the friend and companion of those wandering people known to us under the title of 'gipsies', whose lives are such as necessitate means whereby a 'catch as catch can' existence is an expedient. The lurcher lives in the encampment ... and when food becomes scarce the boiling pot must be filled, and this it will be if the owner of the lurcher has even a shadow of opportunity for doing it.'

Frank Townend Barton, *The Kennel Encyclopaedia*, Virtue, 1930

POACHERS

It is not correct to think of poachers as peasants hunting illegally; much of the latter, in Tudor times especially, was conducted by the gentry themselves.

This implausible strategem would not appeal to most lurchers!
(Charwynne Dog Feature)

Hands-on check.

Good judging is vital.

Six high-quality Show Greyhound bitches from Scandinavia.

JUDGING A LURCHER

It is a strange irony that now that hunting with dogs is so restricted there are more lurchers in the land than ever before. Sadly there are more too in rescue centres than ever before. There are too many being bred – and too many poor specimens being over-praised, and probably then bred from. A few years ago I stood ring-side at a lurcher class during a country show and heard one handler singing the praises of his dog. His words told me more about him than they did about his dog, which wholly lacked the build of an effective hunting dog. It was a not a good lurcher and he was not a good judge of one. A lurcher doesn't have to look statuesque but it has to have the anatomy of a running dog. Historically, if it looked too like a sighthound then the village constable was alerted. But if it couldn't perform like a sighthound then nobody was interested.

'Stonehenge' referred to lurchers well over a hundred years ago with these words: 'A poacher possessing such an animal seldom keeps him long, every keeper being on the look-out, and putting a charge into him on the first opportunity; and as these must occur of necessity, the poacher does not often attempt to rear the dog which would suit him best, but contents himself with one which will not so much attract the notice of those who watch him'. Strictly speaking, on this evidence, a judge at a lurcher show should automatically disqualify any dog which would appear to a gamekeeper like a coursing dog! That would thin out the class sizes in no small way! 'Stonehenge' has managed however to convey the essential ordinariness, the vital anonymity and the lack of type if a lurcher is to survive. Variety was not just the spice of life, it almost assured a life!

This variation in type manifests itself at lurcher shows today, with classes for rough and smooth-haired dogs and those under or over 23 (or 26) inches at the withers. Some breeders swear by the Saluki cross and others by Bedlington blood; some fanciers favour a rough or harsh-haired dog and others the smooth variety. A minority prize the 'Smithfield' blood from the old drovers' dogs and there are often more bizarre crosses such as Beardie Dobermann and Airedale Whippet. The concept, as always with a hunting dog, is to find the ideal match between quarry, country and conditions on one hand and speed, determination and hunting instinct on the other.

The best judge of a lurcher is a man who has hunted one himself, a man who visualises the dog before him in the ring in the chase. But he has to possess some basic knowledge of the fundaments of hunting dog anatomy or he has no right to be in the ring as a judge. I see judges at shows who never look at the feet, never test the hardness of the loin, don't examine the bite, and reward entrants with weak loins, upright shoulders and ribcages which lack lung room. That can only reward bad breeding, leading to a production-line of mediocre dogs; winning dogs get bred from!

Firstly, why are so many lurchers so big? It is worth remembering that the main reason why show Deerhounds tend to be huge is not need but origin. Deer hunters found that dogs over 28 inches at the withers lacked performance and quickly passed them on to the early show breeders. No Waterloo Cup winner has ever been 30 inches high. I regularly see lurchers at shows which stand 30 inches and which must weigh over 80lb. I would have thought that even on Salisbury Plain or around Newmarket, 60 to 70lb was easily big enough. The famous coursing Greyhound Master M'Grath, three times winner of the Waterloo Cup, believed by many to have no equal for pace, cleverness and killing power, weighed 52 to 54lb. Wild Mint weighed 45lb and Coomassie only 42; both were superbly effective coursing dogs.

But whatever their size it is possible to judge these admirable dogs more effectively. If we are going to judge them, let's do it properly. A hound which hunts using its speed must have the anatomy to do so. Immense keenness for work will always come first but the physique to exploit that mental asset comes close second. A lurcher must have a long strong muzzle with powerful jaws and a level bite, with strength right to the nose-end of the muzzle. How else can it catch and retrieve its quarry? The nose should be good-sized with well-opened nostrils, for, despite some old-fashioned theories, sighthounds hunt using scent as well as sight.

For any sighthound to succeed, its eyes should be fairly prominent and be set slightly oblique, to the side of the head. One eye should look away to the right and one to the left so that, like any good rangefinder, both eyes can be used for long distance marking. It is likely however that at close range only one eye is used at a time. The neck should be long but symmetrically so, muscular and firm. Length of neck does not improve 'pick up'; flexibility in the 'swoop' comes from the placement of the shoulder blades.

A lurcher must have well laid back sloping shoulders; I always apply the 'two fingers width' test to the space between the shoulder blades of a stooping dog. Many show Greyhounds have to spread their feet to drink from a bowl of water on the ground because of excessive narrowness in the set of their shoulder blades. The lurcher's back should hint at suppleness and power, be slightly arched in the lumbar region, yet have a mainly level topline. A judge should know the difference between a long back and a long body; a short-bodied long-backed hound is a handicapped one.

The chest should be deep from the withers to point of elbow but be fairly flat, with the underpart of the brisket fairly broad across. The ribs should be well separated, with good lung room and space between the last rib and the hindquarters to allow a full stride. At full stretch, the impress of a hare's hind-feet is implanted in front of that of the forefeet; the lurcher should have the same capability. There must also be freedom of suspension in the ribcage or thorax in the way it is 'cradled' by the scapulae – the dog needs to utilise this when hurdling a farm gate or turning at high speed.

The hindquarters must be powerfully constructed if they are to propel the dog forward in the chase, but symmetry and balance fore and aft are the key to turning ability. Every sighthound depends upfront on good long arms and forearms, and, in the hindlegs wide and muscular thighs and second thighs, length of stifle and good angulation. The feet must be really compact with well-knuckled toes and short claws, naturally worn from working or sound exercise. Some Greyhound experts have been known to assess a dog by looking at the tail first, noting any sign of coarseness, desiring the tail of a rat in appearance, long and whiplike with little hair. I like to examine the pads, seeking even wear on each one.

Smooth-coated lurchers are sometimes handicapped by too thin a coat, lacking protection from wire and chill winds. Whilst not advocating a shaggy wolfhound coat, I can see operational merit in a stiff-haired, wire-haired or linty coat. The jacket of any sporting dog should shed the wet not hold the wet. Waterproofing comes from hair density and texture not profusion of coat; if you look at the originally imported Afghan hounds and then compare their coats to today's specimens, you can see how function has been forfeited to fashion.

Far too many exhibitors at country shows expect the judge to see merit in their entry when they themselves have done little to prepare the exhibit for the ring. Some dogs are natural showmen, most are not. Dogs need to be schooled for the ring – not slavishly prepared, God forbid! but trained to walk briskly on the lead and stand still during closer scrutiny. A future judge's examination of the bite is made easier by previous rehearsal. Why should your dog unquestioningly allow a complete stranger to look inside its mouth? But jaw construction really does matter and a competent judge will always want to check this important feature of a sporting dog. The judge can better apply his judging technique if the exhibitor's ring technique has been practised and the exhibit rehearsed. This can significantly affect placings.

Fault judging is no help to anyone, breeder, owner, the status of the show, the sport of showing itself. Overseas they often list faults according to their seriousness, i.e. disqualifying ones down to merely

Winning lurchers owned by Julie Lowden of Cumbria.

A lurcher judge at work.

undesirable ones. No lurcher should ever win in the ring if it features upright shoulders, short upper arms, a weak neck or loins, poor feet, a short body (especially with a long back) or shoulder blades which touch when the dog stoops to put its nose to the ground. There is no such thing as the perfect dog; it's vital to judge the *whole* dog, not descending on the animal, oozing praise just because it's in superlative condition, has powerful hindquarters or a superb head. The sporting dog needs every part of its body to be sound! In KC show rings far too many breeds are judged solely on their heads or their coats or their flashy gait.

Movement demonstrates soundness, or reveals flawed physiques; the initial overall appraisal can reveal symmetry and allow assessment of the whole dog. The closer hands-on examination allows the slope of shoulder, the strength of loin, the muscular development, the skeletal frame and the construction of the jaw to be checked. But the sequence of the examination is crucial. For me, it is logical to view the whole dog standing and moving *before* a closer look is given. And by moving I mean three dimensional: going away, going across and then heading directly for me. I am seeking effortless locomotion, a balanced harmonious economical gait and no excessive action, either to the side or off the ground. Does the dog look as though it could go on like this for miles?

Any closer examination has, for me, to follow a set sequence: head, jaw, eyes and ears, neck and shoulders together, back and loins together, set of tail and pelvic slope together. Then to the lower case: spread and elbows together, front legs AND feet, thorax and tuck-up, hindlimbs AND feet then coat and character. Judging character isn't straightforward; I go for the look in the eye, the tail action and the confident body language. We all surely want keen willing up-on-their-toes sporting dogs. Without a set sequence I'd be worried I'd miss something. I am always willing to converse with an exhibitor in the ring but am aware of crafty attempts to influence me. I was once told by the owner of a splay-footed, wry-mouthed, surprisingly flabby lurcher that his dog regularly caught hares 'single-handed'. 'But never with his mouth!' was my response!

I am always prepared to discuss my placings with exhibitors at the end of the show; I am always willing to give a view on the 'state of the entry' so that some idea is provided on the overall standard of the dogs shown under me. An average dog winning from a tiny entry should not become overrated. In the end, of course, what the dog can *do* will always be more important than what it looks like. But sound construction will always allow a sporting dog to excel and that is the task of the lurcher judge: to reward soundness, not showiness. Winning dogs get bred from; who wants a kennel full of useless show-offs?

But the best physique is squandered without a well-developed desire to hunt, backed by immense determination; an alert eager expression in the eye indicates this and is essential. A judge has to ask himself: will this dog hunt? Can this dog hunt with this anatomy? Better judging, based on a more measured assessment, should lead to the production of better dogs. Fieldsports folk have too much sense to allow such a concept to degenerate into the 'pretty Polly' state prevalent in the pedigree dog show rings. Lurcher shows are an enjoyable day out; the only real test for such a dog is in the field. But that enjoyable day out can raise standards too if the judges' criteria are sound. Who wants to win with an unworthy dog?

Pace before grace
The Greyhound as a 'show dog' is a failure, rather than otherwise. With few exceptions, the best animals in the field have not possessed that beautiful shape and elegance of contour that is attractive in the ring. Master McGrath was as ugly a dog to look at, from this point of view, as could be imagined; Fullerton is better, but his appearance is by no means taking.

Rawdon Lee, *Modern Dogs: Sporting Division*, Cox, 1897

SELECTING THE BLOOD

Over a century ago, a Gloucestershire breeder, Capt Graham, decided to re-create the real Irish Wolfhound, and, from the skilful use of blended blood, produced the modern breed. He and his knowledgeable fellow-breeder, Major Garnier, established a number of rules for cross-breeding in the pursuit of a fixed type. These are surely of value to any serious lurcher breeder and can be listed as follows.

Quality is much more dependent on the dam than the sire. Muscular development and conformation comes mainly from the dam. Bone and size are more dependent on the sire than the dam. Colour is almost wholly dependent on the sire but coat texture is almost wholly *independent* of the sire. They considered too that all these attributes became modified by any impurity of blood, or, in other words, a lack of line-breeding to 'fix' traits. With hunting so limited nowadays, I do hope that performance won't gradually be relegated and false reputation accepted.

Down the long years of dog breeders seeking better dogs, some breeders have succeeded and some have not. It is important to learn from those successful breeders and benefit from their hard-earned knowledge. It is vital to learn from the very best breeders not those with the best brag or the loudest voices. Raymond Oppenheimer owned the Ormandy Bull Terriers, the most successful kennel of its time, raising the quality level of the whole breed. Unlike so many show breeders he was happy to share his extensive knowledge of breeding with his peers, his twenty key points for success being:

Don't make use of indiscriminate outcrosses, an injudicious one can produce an aggregation of every imaginable fault in the breed.

Only line breed to complementary types, a successful combination could bring great rewards.

Don't take advice from unsuccessful breeders; if their opinions were worth having, they would have proved it by their successes.

Don't believe the popular cliché about the brother or sister of a great champion being just as good to breed from – it depends on the dogs themselves.

Don't be kennel-blind; self-deceit is a stepping stone to failure.

Don't breed from mediocrities; the absence of fault does not in any way signify the presence of its corresponding virtue.

Don't try to line breed to two dogs at the same time, you will end up line breeding to neither.

Don't assess the worth of a stud dog by his inferior progeny, all dogs sire a proportionately large percentage of rubbish; what matters is how good their best efforts are.

Don't allow personal feelings to influence your choice of a stud dog, the right dog for your bitch is the right dog, no matter who owns it.

Don't allow admiration of a stud dog to blind you to his faults.

Don't mate animals which share the same fault, or you are asking for trouble.

Don't forget that it is the whole dog that counts; if you forget one virtue whilst searching for another you will pay for it.

Don't search for the perfect dog as a mate for your bitch, it doesn't exist.

Don't be frightened of breeding from animals that have obvious faults, so long as they have compensating virtues. A lack of virtue is by far the greatest fault of all!

Don't mate together non-complementary types, an ability to recognise type at a glance is a breeder's greatest gift.

Don't forget the necessity to preserve head quality, it will vanish like a dream if you do.

Don't forget that substance, plus quality, should be one of your aims; anyone can breed one without the other.

A great head plus soundness should be your aim.

The supreme canine athlete at full stretch.

At full stretch.

The Greyhound epitomises the Sighthounds.

Don't ever try to decry a great dog... a great dog should be a source of aesthetic pride and pleasure to all true lovers of the breed.

Don't be satisfied with anything but the best, second best is never good enough.

Oppenheimer was a show-dog man but his Bull Terriers triumphed and his breeding methods are reflected in his lasting contribution to the breed. He was helped by having an outstanding kennel man, the great Tom Horner, but he was very much the guiding light. Can lurchermen learn from his words? There is no shortage of lurchers nowadays, the sporting press is full of notices advertising their sale; my local Blue Cross rescue kennel is full of unwanted ones! There are most definitely too many being bred and if there are so many unwanted ones, too many being disposed of too. Are the ones being bred any good?

Breeding sporting dogs is not just a production line, the ingredients of the product really do matter. Temperament in most family-owned dogs is all too often downgraded or overlooked. Biddability is quite often not actively sought in breeding stock, but for the novice sportsman the dog's ability to respond to commands can mean the difference between retaining or disposing. A giant lurcher might suit the braggers but, in these times, who wants to feed a dog which doesn't fill the pot? Bull blood can bring determination, persistence and pluck; unwisely chosen, it can bring with it dog-aggression and great stubbornness. Saluki blood can bring considerable handsomeness but does it produce rabbit-catchers? Deerhound blood can bestow stature but does that suit your country, your quarry, your needs?

In his informative book, *Lurchers and Longdogs* (Standfast Press, 1977), Ted Walsh has written: 'The lurcher must have speed, stamina, brains, courage, nose, soundness and a weatherproof coat. The speed need not be quite that of the Greyhound; indeed, it is the pure speed that tires out the Greyhound so quickly. Stamina is essential to the dog that has to run down his game and repeat the exercise as soon as he has got his tongue in again. Without intelligence the lurcher cannot be trained in obedience; he must have courage to face thorn hedges, wire, rough

going and water; he must have sufficient nose to follow up and retrieve wounded game.' Whether your lurcher is rough or smooth coated, 30 or 22 inches, from Collie, Saluki, Deerhound or Whippet blood, the blend of blood has to meet Ted Walsh's criteria. As always in breeding livestock, the shrewd selection of breeding material brings success; the dog will always be more important than its birth certificate!

'A stud dog is not good just because he is good looking. He must be bred right and not be 'chance got', or his good points will not force themselves on his progeny.'

Jocelyn Lucas, *Pedigree Dog Breeding*, Simpkin, 1925

'The breeder who returns from each show with a new rather than an improved ideal rarely accomplishes anything worthwhile, for vacillation in standards is the direct road to confusion of types and to absolute failure. The rolling stone gathers nothing but hard knocks.'

R E Nicholas, *Principles of Dog Breeding*, Toogood, 1930

'Some men show pedigrees; I show dogs and take the prizes.'

William Graham, *Irish Terrier breeder*, 1905

'The first step in any breeding project is the selection of the female that is to produce one's future stock. That is one of the most important, if not the most important, element in any breeding project is beyond dispute. It has become almost a trite and commonplace saying that the would-be breeder should 'begin with the best'... The fact that the mating of two champions, which has been tried on numerous occasions, has had particularly disappointing results only goes to prove that the conception of 'best' in a breeding and hereditary concept differs from the best in a racing and coursing sense.'

H Edwards Clarke, *The Greyhound*, Popular Dogs, 1965

'...in the choice of a sire it is necessary to avoid any great and sudden change; that is to say, that it seldom answers to put a little, compact, short-working bitch to a great, loose, fast and wide-running dog, unless she is of a much crossed breed, and he is of the reverse, when the result will be that the progeny will follow his mould, and very few of them will resemble the dam.'

John Henry Walsh, *The Pursuit of Wild Animals for Sport*, 1856

Greyhounds are prized for their *speed*.

A Saluki in full gallop.

Generations of breeding for function. Past Waterloo Cup winners

GENETICS AND HYBRIDS

'Lord Orford took a lot of trouble over the breeding of his Greyhounds. He tried every sort of cross, including Italian Greyhounds and English lurchers – the latter of the same type as you still find in use as 'warren dogs' on the big heaths around Thetford. He even tried a bulldog cross. Finally, after seven generations of breeding, he got what were acknowledged to be the best Greyhounds of the time. They had 'small ears, rat tails, and skins almost without hair, together with that innate courage... rather to die than relinquish the chase.'

James Wentworth Day, ***The Dog in Sport***, Harrap, 1938

It is not unusual to see lurchers advertised for sale with a description of their breeding indicated by percentages. In this way for sale notices announce that a litter is on offer as: dam ¼ Deerhound ¾ Bedlington, sire ½ Greyhound ½ Beardie. There is a hint behind such an advertisement that the pups will reflect, each and every one of them, those percentages. But genes don't work like that. Such percentages are of interest but not *directly* of value to the future owner of one of these pups.

The pioneer Bullmastiff breeder, S E Moseley, recorded his formula for breeding as: 'Taking a mastiff bitch and a bulldog I produce a 50/50. A bitch of these I mate to a mastiff dog and give me a 75% mastiff 25% bullbitch, which I mate to a 50/50 dog. A bitch from this litter is 62½% mastiff 37½% bulldog. I mate this to a 50/50 dog, and a bitch from this litter I put to a 62½% mastiff 37½% bulldog which gives me approximately my ideal 60% mastiff 40% bulldog.'

Now read the words of Bateson in his *The Progress of Genetic Research* as long ago as 1906: '...dogs, for example, derived from a cross a few generations back have been spoken of as 1/8 bulldog, or 1/32 pointer blood, and so forth. Such expressions are quite uncritical, for they neglect the fact that the characters may be transmitted separately and that an animal may have only 1/32 of the 'blood' of some progenitor, and yet be pure in one or more of its traits.' Moseley was rather better at percentages than he was at genetics.

It is absurd to expect an individual dog from mixed breeding to reflect in looks and performance the percentages of blood in its genetic composition. It is ridiculous to expect each pup in a litter from mixed breeding to look and perform like its litter-mates. It is scientific nonsense to expect in a litter created by a mating in which 25% of the genes are Bedlington Terrier all the pups resulting to be 25% Bedlington either in looks or performance. There is a random nature to genes which *must* be taken into account. If you breed from good stock you stand a better chance of getting good offspring but it does not rule out the chance of getting the odd duffer.

It is difficult too to judge the success rate of a litter once mature. A potentially brilliant working dog can go to a completely useless trainer/handler. A much more limited dog can go to a really gifted trainer/handler and excel. Which represents the better breeding option? Both dogs come from the same genes. I am suspicious of claims made about one particular sire, one particular dam or one particular mating. We hear about successes not failures; most racehorses mated to big-time winners produce progeny which do not match their deeds. There is however a greater chance of producing winning horses from winning stock; bad luck if you get the one without the 'winning *combination* of genes'!

The hound expert Newton Rycroft made some interesting observations on heredity. He listed what he called 'genetic facts' which included: Light colours in the modern orthodox foxhound have more quality

German Shepherd X Whippet.

17th century lurchers.

An early 19th century sporting scene, sadly by an artist unknown, but one who knew his sporting dogs. This scene includes: a catch-dog (collared, foreground), a sighthound (behind the catchdog's head), a par force hound (behind the catchdog's tail), a waterdog (with stick in its mouth), a large Newfoundland-type of water retriever (behind the waterdog) and scenthounds in the middle ground and in the chase beyond.

JUST THREE GENES

Dr Elaine Ostrander of America's National Human Genome Research Institute has examined the genetic basis of the different breed features appearing in dogs. She found that 80% of the variation between breeds in coat texture and furnishings was explained by differences in just three genes. Different combinations of these result in different mixtures of coat and furnishings. A great deal of variety in dogs can be caused by only a little genetic variation.

RIGHT: **Blend of Borzoi and farm Collie. Germany 1924.**

BELOW: **19th century Greyhound x Bulldog.**

than the dark; the blue descendants of Carmarthen Nimrod 24 had better noses than the non-blue; the black hounds in the high quality Dumfriesshire kennel generally have more quality than the ones with more tan; a Greyhound–Bloodhound mating produced four pups, three looked like the Greyhound and had poor noses and the one that looked like a Bloodhound had an excellent nose; although black and yellow Labradors occur in the same litter, it is the blacks which have proved themselves much more successful in field trials.

When discussing these items he posed more questions than he gave answers. But geneticists have linked coat colour with certain skills and head shape is connected with scenting prowess. The American vet Whitney probably cross-bred more dogs than any other person, and produced more data as a result. One of his aims was to identify what was dominant genetically in the various inherited factors. He found (as did Stockard quite separately) that short legs are dominant over long. He showed that the presence of dew-claws on the hindlegs was dominant over their absence. He found that Greyhounds have a larger heart and liver than other breeds and pass this on.

Whitney found that a cross between the Bloodhound and the Bull Terrier had a far far greater resistance to distemper than either the Bloodhounds or the Bloodhound X Great Danes in his kennel. His first and second crosses between breeds showed better disease resistance than the pure-bred dogs in his kennel. He recorded that the narrow pointed head of the sheepdog is dominant over the broader dished head of the Pointer, that the elongated head of the Greyhound was dominant over the short-faced Bulldog but that the latter was dominant over the Dobermann-type and usually dominant over the Basset hound head. He stated that a narrow chest is dominant over a broad chest, that a screw tail is not linked to the Bulldog head – as many believe still – and that the compact foot is usually dominant over the more open hare foot.

Against that background it would be a great benefit to our bank of knowledge if lurcher breeders were to keep detailed records of their breeding results, not just performance records but facts of genetic interest too. You don't have to be a highly qualified scientist to notice genetic facts; Mendel, the father of modern genetics was not a scientist, but he observed what they could not. Someone like my namesake, the highly successful lurcher breeder, must have noted any manner of valuable points which no scientific experiment would have revealed. Cross-breeding dogs can be much more informative than merely perpetuating a pure breed with a closed gene pool.

Cross-breeding to aid a pure breed, or outcrossing as it is known, is becoming less unthinkable for the more enlightened pedigree dog breeders. It is easy to overlook the fact that all our recognised breeds came to us from cross-breeding. It is often overlooked that the dog insurance companies charge a lower premium for cross-bred dogs than for pure-bred dogs, based on medical cost research. It is nearly always overlooked that covert cross-breeding gave the Rough Collie the Borzoi head and the show Border Collie its more profuse coat from the Rough Collie. It is conveniently forgotten that outcrosses to the Greyhound revitalised the Deerhound and those to the springer helped the Field Spaniel.

Now further outcrosses are being condoned. Some years ago an outcross from the Boxer to a Spitz breed was tried in order to produce erect ears. More recently Boxers have been crossed with corgis to obtain naturally docked tails. In Finland, Pinschers and Schnauzers are being crossed to widen the gene pool. They share common ancestors anyway. KC-registered Otterhounds however are unlikely to be outcrossed to the Welsh Hound as they might have been as pack members. In the USA, purpose-bred Assistance Dogs produce a 40% success rate from cross-bred dogs against 33% for pure-breds.

In-breeding is coming under greater scientific scrutiny as inheritable defects in pedigree dogs increase. Professional breeders of production animals such as cows, pigs, goats, sheep and horses consider that a coefficient of in-breeding of around 9% is risky. One researcher in America found that in dog breeds there is a decline in the average life span of around 7% for every 10% increase in in-breeding.

Dwarfism has been found in Pointer litters at in-breeding coefficients of 13 to 37%, whereas unaffected litters rated 0 to 24%. In a Foxhound pack, the conception rate with sperm of in-bred dogs was 73% against 87% with out-bred ones; average litter size was seven against nine and four against six at weaning. The sperm count was 70 against 36. Swedish pedigree dogs of 60 breeds had an average in-breeding coefficient of 14%.

Lurchers are essentially cross-bred dogs; this gives them an inbuilt virility, but over-reliance on certain favoured sires can reduce even the lurcher gene-pool. Breeder honesty and eternal vigilance is absolutely essential.

'Some Lurchers have a Terrier cross, others may have a dash of Harrier, Pointer or Setter. I knew a dog, whose dam was a pure Irish Water Spaniel, and his sire, I believe, a flat-coated Retriever, that was the most perfect hare poacher I ever saw.'

Hugh Dalziel, *British Dogs*, Upcott Gill, 1888

South African tracking dogs

Hunting dogs from mixed breeding: bred for performance – not appearance.
(Charwynne Dog Features)

Alfred Lord Tennyson with his Deerhound lurcher, depicted in his native Lincoln.
(Charwynne Dog Features)

The Cretan Hound – used as a lurcher in Greece.
(Photo Lavrys, Charwynne Dog Features)

CHAPTER 2

PERFECTING THE BLEND

The Value of Collie Blood
The Value of Deerhound Blood
The Bedlington Input
The Bull Lurcher
The Boar Lurcher
The Wolf Lurcher

Charlie: Tasmanian Smithfield (long-tailed) 1 year.
(Graham Rigby, Campbell Town, Tas. 2003)

North-country cow-herd, 1901, with old-type Beardie.
(Charwynne Dog Features)

Two Smithfield Sheepdogs (and Smooth Collie) on duty in World War I.
(Charwynne Dog Features)

THE VALUE OF COLLIE BLOOD

Most lurcher breeders have long accepted the value of the blood of the Collie in their stock; it could be argued that to qualify as a genuine lurcher the involvement of Collie blood is essential. Twenty years ago, I had two working sheepdogs, i.e. unregistered Border Collies, with distinct sporting dog skills. The bitch was a natural setter; she never once gave a false point. The male dog was a remarkable marker and accomplished retriever, with a soft mouth and a willingness to go through any sort of cover. Their eagerness to work was commendable; their obedience constant; their astuteness remarkable. They did of course lack the sheer style of specialist gundogs but a more skilful trainer/handler than I could have developed them to a high standard. This combination of biddability, cleverness and an unquenchable desire to work has led to the use of Collies in a wide variety of ways in the sporting field.

In his book *The Scottish Deerhound* of 1892, Weston Bell summarised a report from the various deerstalking estates of that time which covered the use of dogs on them. The extracts he prints are illuminating: Achanault Deer Forest – no deerhound ever used, Auchnashellach, Collie breed – good-nosed tracker. Balmoral Deer Forest – very seldom do we use the staghounds – only keep them for breeding with the Collie. Inverwick Forest – very few gentlemen use deerhounds nowadays in the forest – only the half-bred dogs, between the Collie and Retriever. Fairley Deer Forest – one Collie in use now. One formerly. Deerhounds are not used in any deer forest that I know of in the north of Scotland. The best dog I ever saw for tracking a wounded stag was a cross between a Retriever and a pure Collie. Collie dogs, when trained young, turn out excellent trackers. Inchgrundle – Collie dogs have been chiefly used here for deerstalking during the last twenty years. We generally find the Collie more useful than the staghound.

The widespread use of the Collie and the tributes paid to its prowess are astonishing and many other estates stressed their value and sporting skills: Braemore Deer Forest – I consider a good Collie as far superior to any other kind of dog for a wounded deer. Aviemore Deer Forest – three Collies are at present in use... Properly-trained sheep dogs are the best. Mamore Forest – for tracking deer I think no dog so good as a good Collie. Conaglen – we use sheepdogs here – they are more obedient and have more sense than the others. Rothiemurchus Deer Forest – good tracking Collies are the best for deerstalking. Glenartney – good Collies are the best I ever saw. Twenty other estates used Collies for deerstalking.

Three estates used a Collie–Deerhound cross, one used a setter–Collie cross and another chiefly used 'a Collie of the grey shaggy breed', the beardie type. These extensive tributes to Collie blood came from men who worked in the most testing country, in the most trying weather conditions and on a quarry never easy to stalk. The role demanded dogs that were hardy, had great stamina, immense perseverance and responded to commands often over some distance. There was not one mention in this wide-ranging estate survey of Bloodhounds, famous for their noses. The humble Collie was the favoured dog. The Retriever–Collie cross came next. The Collie–Deerhound cross was clearly used in Deerhound lines, before Deerhound to Deerhound breeding was restored.

The Collie–Setter cross was allegedly used by the Duke of Gordon in the development of his breed of setters. S E Shirley, the Flat-coat pioneer, bred three of the most famous ancestors of the show Collie – from an Irish Setter–Collie cross. There is a distinct Collie-look to many setters portrayed by artists in the 19th century. Iris Coombe, in her book *Herding Dogs*, relates how French sportsmen took their Brittanys to Scottish sporting estates and were so impressed by the cleverness of the local Collies that they mated their dogs to them. They would have been seeking intelligence, trainability and responsiveness. Around 1826, the Marquis of Huntley angered the Setter owners using Findhorn by utilising the clever Collie of a local gamekeeper/shepherd as a sire for his Setters. He put brains before beauty and got much abuse for it.

In his *The Dog* of 1887, the celebrated writer 'Stonehenge' observed: 'When the lurcher is bred from the rough Scotch Greyhound and the Collie, or even the English sheep-dog, he is a very handsome dog, and even more so than either of his progenitors when pure... A poacher possessing such an animal seldom keeps him long, every keeper being on the look-out, and putting a charge of shot into him on the first opportunity.' He went on to state that poachers made great efforts to avoid their lurchers *looking like* just that, to avoid being shot. But it has to be said that another reason, down the years, for antipathy towards Collie cross lurchers in country areas, quite apart from poaching, is that the Collie blood can contribute to an undesired canine interest in mutton!

Ted Walsh, in his *Lurchers and Longdogs* states that to create his sort of lurcher, he would start with two Collie bitches, mate one to a Greyhound and the other to a Deerhound. The resultant pups would be fully tested and then culled, the survivors being inter-bred. The progeny of this mating would then be put back to a coursing Greyhound. This would have given him a preponderance of Greyhound blood but a fair input of Collie blood too. It is absurd to declare precise percentages in products of mixed blood; genes work in a random way, not mathematically. Old lurcher breeders tended to put sagacity ahead of raw speed. The sighthound breeds are not renowned for their obedience or their brains; Collies are.

Old lurcher breeders, too, prized the blood of the Smithfield Collie, a type fast disappearing from the lurcher scene, in numbers at least. The leggy hairy Smithfield sheepdog has never been conserved here as such, but in Tasmania, Graham Rigby has some splendid specimens. Just as the Australian stumpy-tailed cattle dog is a descendant of the dogs once common in Cumberland, and still are so in the Black Mountain area near Hereford, these Tasmanian dogs originated here. Graham has had the breed for over twenty years. The first Smithfields to go to Australia were called black bobtails, big rough-coated square-bodied dogs, with heads like wedges, a white frill round the neck and 'saddleflap' ears. Graham is not a lurcher man, but any lurcher breeder seeking this blood might find the expense of obtaining his stock worth every penny.

In his *Hunters All* of 1986, Brian Plummer paid tribute to the Collie lurchers of my namesake and Phil Lloyd. David's publication *Lambourn* of some twenty years ago contains some of the best Collie lurcher photos I have ever seen, well worth a study. What you see there is not a flashy show poseur but a functional creature bred for work. They remind me of the clever Collie lurchers worked by the gypsies near my boyhood home. These dogs were trained to catch game at first and last light, hide it, and then retrieve it during darkness. I don't recall any of their owners being prosecuted for poaching. These gypsies only bred from their own stock.

Of course, you can get brainless Collies, and long-backed short-bodied ones, leading to weak loins, a bad feature in a lurcher, and sometimes a lack of lung-room too; not good in a running dog. In addition, some Collies are just too hyperactive to be valuable sporting dogs. Selection of breeding stock will always be the key to the successful production of lurchers, not the mix of ingredients. The dogs favoured for use in the Scottish deer forests were not valued because they were Collies or Collie crosses, but because they were outstanding dogs. If you want a dog with brains, biddability and a zeal for work, the Collie offers all three. Every employer surely values a zeal for work!

'I think it is difficult to improve on the first cross Beardie/Border or Beardie/Border cross-bred. These I believe to be the best knock about, all round lurchers with ample speed, reasonable intelligence, excellent tractability and a really tough constitution. I am however open to comments about both half-bred and 3/4 Collie 1/4 Greyhound hybrids.'

Brian Plummer, *Sporting News*, 1989

'The Lurcher proper is a cross between the Scotch Colley and the Greyhound. An average one will stand about three-fourths the height of the Greyhound. He is more strongly built than the latter dog, and heavier boned, yet lithe and supple withal; his whole conformation gives an impression of speed...'

Hugh Dalziel, *British Dogs*, Upcott Gill, 1888

The lurcher intentionally cross-bred: this one is Smithfield Collie x Greyhound.
(Charwynne Dog Features)

Classic lurcher ingredient: Working Collie of 1904 from Lundy Island.

BELOW: **Ellis Hughes, a shepherd at Glasfryn, Clwyd, with two Welsh Grey Sheepdogs and a Fox Terrier, the latter a farm vermin-controller.**
(courtesy Museum of Welsh Life)

Scenes from Sir Samuel Baker's book on hunting in Ceylon.

**Deerhound lurcher or
'Staghound' lurcher.**
(Charwynne Dog Features)

THE VALUE OF DEERHOUND BLOOD

The blood of the Deerhound has long been prized by knowledgeable lurcher men. Many sportsmen are most impressed by their hunting skills and quite remarkable facility for detecting movement over huge distances. They can track as well as hunt by sight. Some breeds have changed in the hands of show breeders but this breed seems to have retained its essential type over several centuries. It is easy to overlook the value of hounds which could hunt red deer successfully before the wide use of long range firearms. In a harsh winter the skill of such a dog could mean the difference between starvation and survival for the primitive hunters. Once this value diminished however, these huge shaggy fast-running hounds fell on hard times, surviving only in some areas through the patronage of the nobility. Pennant recorded, when visiting Scotland in 1769, that he saw at Gordon Castle true Highland Greyhounds which had become very scarce. He described these hounds as 'of large size, strong, deep-chested, and covered with very long and rough hair', used 'in large numbers at the magnificent stag chases by the powerful chieftains.' Lurcher men, keepers and stalkers refer to them as staghounds to this day.

The Earl de Folcoville had his noted Colonsay strain in the first half of the 19th century. MacNeile, in his chapter on Deerhounds, the first detailed write-up of the breed, in Scrope's book on deerstalking of 1838, described 'Buskar', one of the purest specimens, as 28 inches at the *shoulder*, with a chest girth of 32 inches, weighing 85lb, going on to write: 'This dog is of pale yellow, and appears to be remarkably pure in his breeding, not only from his shape and colour, but from the strength and wiry elasticity of his hair, which by Highlanders is thought to be a criterion of breeding.' MacNeile stated that the grey dogs appeared to be 'less lively and did not exhibit such a development of muscle, particularly on the back and loins, and have a tendency to cat hams'.

The classic use of Deerhounds involves a brace coursing their quarry and killing it unaided. This demands not just speed, strength and stamina but superbly constructed dogs, whose limbs and, especially, feet can cope with boulder-strewn terrain at great speed, whose joints can withstand fierce jarring and whose physique combines great power with lightness of build. The first point my eye seeks out in a moving Deerhound, even in a show ring, is a noticeable springiness of step and 'daisy-clipping' action in the feet; for me all other points are subordinate to this essential feature. It reveals soundness.

I haven't seen the attractive red coat colouration for many many years but I have seen some fine blue–grey specimens down the years. I get depressed when I see Deerhounds in the show ring with woolly coats, poor feet and no spring in their gait, lacking leg muscle and depth of chest. This breed is descended from a primitive hunting dog, prized for its field prowess, famed for its strength and speed and essentially a functional animal. I get concerned too about Deerhounds being bred for great size at the expense of soundness; for the breed standard to stipulate a *minimum* height of 30 inches at the withers for dogs and 28 inches for bitches, with no mention of soundness first and foremost, is to my mind, unwise.

In a pedigree breed with a closed gene pool a loss of stature becomes increasingly likely with each decade. I would much rather have an overall sound dog of 28 inches at the withers than an oversized unsound dog. An inch or two in stature can never match the overall soundness so essential in a hunting dog. Deerhound blood has been utilised not just by lurcher men in Britain but by their opposite numbers hunting coyotes in America and kangaroo in Australia. Such breeders are seeking all round hunting skills: a good nose, coursing ability and the keen determination to pursue a fast quarry over some distance.

The Deerhound is considered to be the brightest of the sighthounds, some say handed down from the Collie blood used many years ago. But just as Deerhound blood is of value in outcrosses, so too may, for example, Greyhound blood be needed once again in the Deerhound breed, for the genetic base is small. Pure breeding is fine when things are going well but disastrous when inbred faults such as weak hindquarters are being perpetuated.

It is likely that the Deerhound has retained its essential type because it seems to attract distinguished owners and breeders. Names like Miss Doxford of the Ruritania kennel, the Misses Loughrey of the Ross kennel, Miss Bell of the Enterkine kennels, Miss Linton (Geltsdale), Miss Hartley (Rotherwood) and Miss Noble (Ardkinglas) would grace any breed club register. But I do see, mainly over the last decade, far too many Deerhounds in a new mould: small, woolly-coated and light in bone, with sharp pointed heads and completely lacking the soft eye. Hounds like this are really without true type.

Writing in his *Dogs of Scotland*, published in 1891, Thomson Gray remarked that: 'Another great drawback in connection with deerhounds is that they become small and weedy through interbreeding...all breeders will acknowledge that it is a serious one'. Nobody wants the Deerhound to have the narrow head of the Borzoi or Greyhound but if this pedigree breed does need an infusion of new blood there are some fine Deerhound type lurchers around, although far too many of the latter are rather coarse-headed and often over-boned.

Show ring Deerhounds nowadays can display poor toplines, short upper arms, slab-sided chests and a lack of underline. Although hip dysplasia is not a common problem in the breed, osteochondritis, and torsion of the stomach, spleen and lung have been recorded. Lurchermen utilising Deerhound blood would be wise to obtain health checks before investing in breeding material. Stature too in this breed should be based on their hunting feats and never on sheer size alone; this is a fine sporting breed not an ornament.

Critiques on Deerhounds in the show ring in 2007 included these faults: too many light eyes, large ears and upright fronts, weak pasterns, splayed fronts, weak quarters and a lack of muscle, lack of spring of rib, poorly knuckled feet, poor front assemblies – with elbows in front of chests and untypically wide behind. This is not encouraging. If I were going to buy a Deerhound, I'd get one from the Doxhope kennels of Bill Doherty. A respect for the function of a hound, however distant, is the way to breed a sound animal, more today than any day in the past, as hunting becomes a mere memory.

In her valuable book on the breed, Nora Hartley, who bred the famous Rotherwood hounds, ends with these words: 'Stock-breeding is like a marathon – we take the torch from the hand of the past, do all that in us lies to carry it forward and pass it, still bravely flaring, into the grasp of the future. So let us do so for deerhounds.' Those wise words should be the leitmotiv for every Deerhound breeder during their time in the breed. Producing puppies is the task of the dam; producing sound typical Deerhounds is the task for the breeder, with any true devotee keeping the faith rather than lamely following the style of the day. All breeds are at the mercy of show ring whims but the ancient breeds merit our vigilance and care. In future this may well become more and more difficult, as owners increasingly seek dogs which have no function and merely satisfy their preferred appearance. There is a challenge here.

The noted Deerhound and Deerhound-lurcher breeder, Bill Doherty, has written that 'My pure-bred deerhounds, although never possessing the ability to match the sheer versatility of their cross-bred relations, have also achieved a certain degree of all-round hunting success.' If both your quarry and country demand a big rough-coated sighthound, then Deerhound blood has a great deal going for it.

From *The Book of Field Sports* by Henry Miles 1864.

Without a function a breed gets lost.

A Deerhound, 1826, Landseer. (Charwynne Dog Features)

Working Bedlington Terrier.

Italian Water Dog.
(Charwynne Dog Features)

SHOW BEDLINGTONS OF 1900
Lurcher breeders resorting to the blood of show Bedlingtons should note the words of the 2009 Crufts judge for this breed: 'I am greatly concerned at the lack of quality currently being shown... Bedlingtons should not be short-coupled, a few had very narrow fronts; poor hind movement was prevalent.' (Charwynne Dog Features)

THE BEDLINGTON INPUT

The breed title of Bedlington Terrier does scant justice to such a capable all-round hunting dog; if anything the Bedlington is a pedigree lurcher, whose blood is much valued by lurcher men. As a breed, the ancestry of the Bedlington is, relative to most breeds, well documented and free from myths. From the celebrated hunt terriers, Peacham and Pincher, of Edward Donkin of Rothbury to the nailors' terriers in the Northumbrian village of Bedlington itself, from Joseph Ainsley's dog and Christopher Dixon's bitch and their offspring, the prototype Piper and Coate's Phoebe, came the foundation of the breed. Mention is sometimes made of the use of blood from small Otterhounds, Bull Terriers and an infusion of Whippet too, in the development of the breed. But little reference is made to the origin of the distinctive topknot, the highly individual linty coat and the range of self-colours in the breed.

There was a dog with a topknot and a tight linty-twisty coat in light liver on the Berwick coast and up into the Cheviot Hills at the time the early types of Rothbury Forest Dog were emerging. It was known locally as the Tweed Water Spaniel, but Tweed Water Dog would have been more accurate. Water Spaniels have the marcelled coat texture, as the American Water Spaniel illustrates. Water Dogs have the 'poodle-coat' as the Italian, the Spanish and the Portuguese Water Dogs demonstrate. Water Dogs have long been favoured by the gypsy community, with gypsy families like the Jeffersons, the Andersons and the Faas, living in the Rothbury Forest at the start of the 19th century. They were famous for their terriers, long-dogs and water dogs. I believe that the distinctive coat of the Bedlington comes from a water dog origin.

In the 19th century, a show held by the old British Kennel Association featured a water-rescue competition, which was won, not surprisingly, by a Newfoundland. But a Bedlington won the third prize and was equal second in the speed trial. In a letter to *The Field* in 1869, a correspondent stated that 'the Bedlington Terrier is fast, and whether on land or water is equally at home'. In his valuable book *Sporting Terriers* Pierce O'Conor wrote that 'Bedlingtons are invariably fine water dogs and have wonderful noses. They are the ideal waterside hunters...' From Squire Trevelyan's Old Flint, a dog whelped in 1782, we have inherited over the last two centuries a unique breed of sporting dog, with earthdog instincts and a race-track capability. It is hardly surprising to find lurchermen valuing their blood. They can look like lambs but perform like lions.

Bedlingtons from working lines can look very different from their show ring counterparts, where over-coiffeuring can spoil the appearance of what is essentially a sporting breed. Breed devotees like Ken Bounden have striven to minimise this, whilst working line advocates like George Newcombe, Harry Marsden, Les White, Stuart Staley and Margaret Williamson long warned against too much beautification. My main worry however is not the coat but the curve! The breed's back has a natural arch over the loin, but it is vital that this is over the loin and not further forward, affecting the power of the dog's movement. This breed must gallop with the whole body and never feature a short back. The arch over the loin is balanced by the tuck-up on the underside, giving a distinct sighthound look to the breed.

The coat colour is officially blue, liver or sandy, with or without tan, but I see blacks at country shows and whites at foreign shows. All five of these gene pool colours are classic water dog colours. It is of interest that a misalliance between a Sealyham bitch and a Bedlington has produced four pups, rather like the old Rothbury type Bedlingtons. Two were blue and tan and the other two blue; not one was mainly white, like the Sealyham. The early blues in the breed were described as blue–black. Blue is the dominant colour, liver is recessive. We seem to have lost the rich tan once in the breed, perhaps when so many blue and tans were exported in the 1930s out of prejudice against them here. The 'Gutch Common' coat of Margaret Williamson's kennel was once famous in the breed for its harshness and waterproof qualities.

What does the Bedlington bring to lurchers possessing their blood? Unusually in a terrier breed the Bedlington has the hare-foot, but can also suffer from cracked pads, a hereditary defect indicated by corny outgrowths and deep fissures on the pads themselves, not exactly desirable in a running dog. Copper toxicosis has blighted the Bedlington breed, but to their credit, the show breeders are striving to reduce its incidence.

They can also bring a weatherproof coat and the feisty terrier temperament, although Brian Plummer has written: '...the Bedlington Terrier is a far cry from the tigerish terriers described by Rawdon Lee or the do-or-die terriers bred by Ainsley.' Ted Walsh once wrote: 'An owner of working Bedlingtons has to use tact at all times and avoid situations where jealousy can lead to fighting.'

In a letter to the sporting press some thirty years ago, Brian Plummer also wrote: 'Three generations of 'Pools of Glenridding', Anthony, John and Eddie, always resorted to mating their fell terriers to game Bedlingtons to incease the courage and determination of their dogs... Dobson of the Eskdale and Ennerdale Foxhounds used chocolate-coloured Bedlington terriers to mate his strain of fell terriers.' But some lurcher breeders favour Bedlington blood because it blends well with Whippet blood, the latter taking some of the feistiness away perhaps, the resultant lurcher is a silent worker, not giving tongue when in pursuit of quarry. The gypsies who lived near my boyhood home usually mated lurcher to lurcher, but brought in Bedlington blood about every fifth generation to 'get the poaching dog'! But as always when breeding animals it is the selection of stock which decides; you mate your precious bitch to a chosen sire not to its breed.

A lurcher from a Whippet–Bedlington Terrier cross.
(Charwynne Dog Features)

A Bedlington in working trim.
(Charwynne Dog Features)

TOP LEFT: **Bedlington terrier of the 1950s**
ABOVE: **Today's Show Bedlington.** (Dalton)
LEFT: **Tommy Dobson and two of his terriers hunting on Muncaster Fell.** (From a photograph by Miss M G Fane)

Pit Bull Terrier x Greyhound.
(Charwynne Dog Features)

'Barney', Ian Cuthbertson's bull lurcher.
(Charwynne Dog Features)

Hunting Mastiff: Bullenbeisser (18th century) – the bull lurcher of Germany.

THE BULL LURCHER

'...a breed of Deerhounds were long preserved at Godmersham and Eastwell in Kent, the strain of which went back to Elizabethan days. A good one always pinned the deer by the ear, a criterion of the purity of the strain. They were cream or fawn-coloured, with dusky muzzles, Greyhound speed and half-Greyhound, half-mastiff-like heads... resembling boarhounds in Snyder's or Velasquez's pictures.'

Those words from Lord Ribblesdale's *The Queen's Hounds* described what might be termed heavy hounds or hunting mastiffs. Today some of the Bull Lurchers being bred closely resemble these dogs. In *Bridleways Through History* Lady Apsley wrote that: 'Charles IX received a present of some 'great hounds' from Queen Elizabeth, referred to as 'mastiffs' or 'dogues'...used in France for killing wolves after the levriers d'attache les avaient coiffes' (i.e. after the sighthounds got them by the ear).

In Old English the word docga referred to a mastiff-like dog and has survived as dogue (French), dogo (Argentine-Spanish), dogge (German) and dogg (Swedish). The Deutsche Dogge is the Great Dane; the Englische Dogge was famed as a hunting mastiff in medieval Europe. The Saxon word bandogge, used in Middle English, referred to a leashed hunting mastiff, not a tied-up yard-dog. The word mastiff, now mainly used to describe the breed of Mastiff in England, was not in common use until the early 18th century. It was used loosely to describe any huge dog, not a distinct breed-type. The word mastiff is now agreed to derive from an original source meaning of mixed breeding.

Inevitably the loss of function once the hunting of big game with hounds lapsed led to the disappearance of many types of heavy hound: the Bullenbeisser in Germany, the Mendelan in Russia and the Suliot Dog in Macedonia/Greece, for example. The huge staghounds of Devon and Somerset, disbanded early in the last century, were 27 inches (0.68m) high and described by Dr Charles Palk Collyns in his *The Chase of the Wild Red Deer* as 'A nobler pack of hounds no man ever saw. They had been in the country for years, and had been bred with the utmost care for the express purpose of stag-hunting... their great size enabled them to cross the long heather and rough sedgy pasturage of the forest without effort or difficulty.'

In his valuable book *Hunting and Hunting Reserves in Medieval Scotland*, John Gilbert writes of references to mastiffs in the Scottish Forest Laws; capable of attacking and pulling down deer, they wore spiked collars and were used to attack wolves and hunt boar, when they hunted to the horn. Gilbert was referring to a heavy hound not what is now the modern breed of Mastiff, whose appearance and especially its movement is scarcely houndlike. This makes a point for me. Directly you stop breeding a dog to a known function, even one long lapsed, then the breed that dog belongs to loses its way. We saw this in the Bulldog and now see it increasingly in the broad-mouthed dogs, worryingly too short in the muzzle and progressively less athletic. Their fanciers forget the sporting origins of their breed, foolishly to my mind, and pursue obsessions with heads, bone and bulk. This is not only historically incorrect but is never to the benefit of the dog.

The mastiff breeds, whether huge like the Mastiff of England, as small as the Bulldog of Britain, cropped-eared like the Cane Corso of Italy and the Perro de Presa of the Canaries, loose-skinned like the Mastini of Italy or dock-tailed like the Boerboel of South Africa, are not only fine examples of powerful but good-tempered dogs but form part of their respective nation's canine heritage. It is vital that they do not fall victim to show ring faddists or misguided cliques of rosette-chasing, over-competitive zealots. Today's breeders need to wake up to such unacceptable excesses, honour the proud heritage of these distinguished breeds and respect them for what they

Bull lurcher. (Charwynne Dog Features)

Bull lurcher of 1834.

BELOW: **Lord Brownlow's Bull Terriers in Ireland in 1831: used as Bull lurchers.**

are: the light heavyweights of the canine world, quick on their feet and devastating at close quarter protection when threatened. Such magnificent canine athletes deserve the very best custodianship, with every fancier respecting their hound ancestry, remembering their bravery at man's behest and revering their renowned stoicism.

Whatever the blend of blood behind a Bull Lurcher, the anatomical requirements are similar for this type of hunting dog: a powerful neck, a seizing jaw, with breadth right down to the nose, strong loins, good spring of rib, with the rib-cgae showing good length as well as circumference, immense power in the sprint and great muscularity. Mentally, such a dog has to have considerable persistence, immense determination when closing with quarry yet always be responsive to commands. In the wrong hands such a dog is capable of being misused or not being satisfactorily under control. In today's society, a powerful hunting dog, allowed to be too dominant or inadequately trained, is going to be troublesome.

The awesome catch-dogs depicted by Snyder and Desportes simply cannot fit in with 21st century living in Britain. Breeders of Bull Lurchers need to be wise and socially aware, concentrating on highly biddable dogs and avoiding the production of hyper-aggressive specimens. The Bull Lurcher perpetuates a long line in powerful hunting dogs; their breeders need to respect this as well as the constraints of modern living.

'The best of Lord Orford's strain were purchased by Colonel Thornton on the death of the breeder, and thus found their way from Norfolk to Yorkshire... we are told that 'it was unanimously agreed by all the sportsmen present, that they ran with a great deal of energetic exertion, and always at the hare; that though beaten they did not go in, or exhibit any symptoms of lurching or waiting to kill. These qualifications – pluck and endurance – were no doubt the result of the Bull cross alluded to...'

Vero Shaw, *The Illustrated Book of the Dog*, Cassell, 1879

Bull lurcher of today.
(Charwynne Dog Features)

Boar lurchers in Germany.
(late 18th-century)

Long-eared scent-hounds could bay the boar but only catch-dogs would close with it.

17th-century boar-hunting scene depicting the coarsely-bred matins or saurude, boar-lurchers in our nomenclature, baying the boar before the catch-dog seized the quarry.

Boar lurchers at work, 1710. The boar lurcher was listed in the Linnaean catalogue of 1792, given the title *canis laniarius fuillus* and described as having a strong head and 'lank' hindquarters.

THE BOAR LURCHER

Big game hunting became almost an obsession with some Victorian sportsmen, with some wealthy hunters spending enormous sums and huge amounts of time at this pastime. Sir Samuel Baker describes in his book *The Rifle and the Hound in Ceylon* the use of various dogs in big game hunting. He took a pack of thoroughbred Foxhounds there with him from England, but only one survived a few months' hunting in Ceylon. He favoured, for elk-hunting, a cross between the Foxhound and the Bloodhound, using fifteen couple, supported by lurchers.

Baker stated that the great enemy of any pack was the leopard, which would leap down on stray or isolated hounds and kill them. Baker was fond of 'deer-coursing', the pursuit of axis or spotted deer using Greyhound and horse. He used pure Greyhounds, 'of great size, wonderful speed and great courage.' A buck could weigh 250lb and would turn and charge its pursuers, unlike the elk which stood at bay. With some sadness he wrote that 'the end of nearly every good seizer is being killed by a boar. The better the dog the more likely he is to be killed, as he will be the first to lead the attack, and in thick jungle he has no chance of escaping from a wound.' The boar lurcher has never received the recognition it merits.

It would be good to see appropriate recognition for the boar lurchers or hunting mastiffs, whether described as docgas, bandogges, seizers, holding dogs, pinning dogs, perro de presas, filas, bullenbeissers or leibhunde. They should at least be respected for their past bravery and bred to the design of their ancestors. A big game hunting breed like the Mastiff of England seems prized nowadays solely for its weight and size. The Englische Dogge (dogge meaning mastiff) was once famous throughout central Europe as a hunting mastiff par excellence. It is a fact that, in the boar-hunting field in central Europe in the period 1500 to 1800, many more catch-dogs were killed than the boars being hunted. In those days there was a saying in what is now Germany that if you wanted boars' heads you had to sacrifice dogs' heads.

Many types of dog have been used in the boar-hunt, with only one modern breed, the Great Dane or German Mastiff, directly inheriting the boarhound mantle. Hounds of the pack were often regarded as too precious to be risked in the final moments of the boar-hunt, so more coarsely bred dogs were used 'at the kill', being considered expendable. These were variously described as catch-dogs, bandogges, alauntes and seizers. They were recklessly brave, remarkably agile, extraordinarily determined and admirably athletic. A better name for them would be 'boar lurchers'; they were never intended to be a breed, they were never uniformly bred and nearly always owned by the lower classes, who were sometimes paid or rewarded for doing so, as a contribution to the hunt.

In England, in the reign of Henry the Second, the wild boar was hunted with hounds and spears in many wooded areas, from the Forest of Dean to Warwickshire and beyond. King James hunted the boar at Windsor, this being described as 'a more dangerous amusement than it was likely he could find any pleasure in'. Turbervile, writing in the late 16th century, recorded that hounds accustomed to running the boar were spoiled for game of scent less strong. They were alleged to be less inclined to stoop to the scent of deer or hare and disinclined to pursue a swifter quarry which did not turn to bay when out of breath. The East India Company introduced hunting dogs from England into India in 1615; on one occasion a mastiff from England shamed 'the Persian dogs' at a boar kill.

In central Europe there were once huge dogs used in the boar-hunts of the great forests of what is now Germany, western Poland and the Czech

Republic. They were known as 'hatzruden' (literally big hunting dogs), huge rough-haired cross-bred dogs, supplied to the various courts by peasants. They were the 'expendable' dogs of the boar-hunt, used at the kill. The nobility however bred the smooth-coated 'sauruden' (boar hounds), and 'saupacker' (literally, member of a pack used for hunting wild boar). The 'saufanger' (boar seizer) was the catch-dog or hunting mastiff.

The 'sauruden' were the equivalent, in the late 18th century, of the hunting alaunts of the 15th century, with the Bullmastiff being the modern equivalent of the 'Alaunts of the butcheries' (see p54 for a description of Alaunts). The specialist 'leib-hund', literally 'body-dog', was the catch-dog used to close with the boar and seize it. I believe it is perfectly reasonable to regard the modern breed called the Great Dane (in English-speaking countries) or Deutsche Dogge (German mastiff) as the inheritor of the saurude or boar hound mantle.

The true boar hound, a hound of the chase or chien courant, as opposed to a huge cross-bred dog once used at the killing of the boar, deserves our respect. Such a hound was required to pursue and run down one of the most dangerous quarries in the hunting field. It needed to be a canine athlete, have a good nose, great determination and yet not be too hot-blooded. Both the Fila Brasileiro and the Dogo Argentino have been used in the boar-hunt in South America. American Bulldogs are still used as catch-dogs on feral pig in the USA, with Bullmastiff crosses being favoured in New Zealand.

In our modern so-called more tolerant society, such powerful determined hunting dogs are stigmatised and even banned in some allegedly liberal countries. Paradoxically the most wide-ranging ban has been imposed in a country whose citizens have carried out the worst atrocities in modern history. These are not happy times for hunting dogs bred by man to be determined, strong and recklessly brave. Sadly, they are also irreplaceable. Prized for several millennia for their dash and bravery, powerful sporting dogs are now under suspicion just because they are powerful. We may not want strapping courageous dogs to pull down big game for us any more

but they are part of our sporting heritage and deserve our support. We never lacked support from them.

The great forests of central Europe provided endless opportunities for hunting. In the 19th century the pursuit of wild animals with hounds was conducted on a vast scale. In France there were over 350 packs of hounds. In 1890 the Czar of Russia organised a grand fourteen-day hunt in which his party killed 42 European bison, 36 elk and 138 wild boar. In many of these hunts, scenthounds, sighthounds, running mastiffs or par force hounds (the true gazehounds) and hunting mastiffs (often held on the leash until needed at the kill and called 'bandogges' by the Saxons) were used in the same hunt.

The ancient Greeks, Gaston Phoebus in the 14th century, the Bavarians in the 17th century and the Czars in the 19th century used hunting dogs of different types in unison according to function. Sighthounds, scenthounds and hunting mastiffs were used *together* and not hunted separately, unlike our more specialist packs. Boarhounds could therefore be the loose term to describe all hounds on a boar-hunt, whatever their function in the chase and kill. Casual researchers can therefore look at a painting of a boar-hunt or read accounts of one and jump to all sorts of false conclusions about what boarhounds could look like in past times.

The invention of firearms brought not just dramatic advantages to hunter-sportsmen but a substantially reduced risk to their lives. This very much lessened their dependence, in some forms of hunting, on determined courageous dogs. We live in times when powerful dogs brave enough to tackle boar, bull and bison are banned in some countries, not because of any current misdeeds, but purely because of their past as a type of dog. In modern times too a dog that can singlehandedly catch a hare is valued less than a dog that can only retrieve a dead rabbit. Until the writings of Phil Drabble and then Brian Plummer redressed the situation, whole libraries were devoted to dogs only capable of retrieving dead game whilst books on lurchers and catch-dogs were as rare as a sighthound in jungle country.

ABOVE: **Boar-hunt in Albania 100 years ago: these boar lurchers would bay a boar but not seize it.**

LEFT: **English Hunting Mastiffs at work. The sporting artist Lionel Edwards' illustration of medieval big-game hunting with the Hunting Mastiffs.**

We may not *want* our Bulldogs to seize big game but they should still be built to do so.

A number of enthusiasts have and still are attempting to recreate the medieval type known as Alaunts, of which there were three main types: one resembled a strong-headed sighthound, another the Great Dane and a third the classic 'butchers' or holding dog, rather like the Bullmastiff. To seek to recreate a breed called the Alaunt involves the production of a type spanning say the Greyhound, the Cane Corso and the Bulldog; that would be some achievement. It would be just as difficult to restore the bandogge as a distinct breed and there is comparable confusion about this type. Even as diligent an author as Robert Leighton, in Edwardian times, took the view that the name bandogge or tie-dog referred to a secured guard dog. Sadly most of the revered Victorian writers on dogs cribbed from each other and in so doing cemented myths through sheer repetition. The words of Barnabe Googe in the 16th century linked the word bandogge with a tied-up house dog and, no doubt such a formidable dog made an effective protector of the house – and needed tying up!

Rather than a tethered yard-dog, I believe there is ample evidence to indicate that the bandogge was a seizing dog, leashed during the hunt, until required as a catch-dog, to grip or hold big game which has been chased to near-exhaustion by the running mastiffs, of Great Dane type. This is a time-honoured way of hunting big game with powerful hounds, as the Assyrian bas-relief demonstrates. The 'band' or tie retains the savage dogs until the moment they are needed to risk their lives at the behest of man. There are countless portrayals of this in medieval paintings and engravings. There is an old English ballad of around 1610 which includes the lines: 'Half a hundred good band-dogs, Came running over the lee.' There is little indication of solitary tied-up yard-dogs in those words.

The Alaunts were the dogs of the Alans. The Alans were astounding horsemen, so rated as to provide the cavalry for the Roman legions. In a well-known inscription, found at Apta on the Durance, the Emperor Hadrian praises and commemorates his 'Borysthenes Alanus Caesareus Veredus' that 'flew' with him over swamps and hills in Tuscany, as he hunted the wild boar. The Romans hunted the wild boar with hunting mastiffs; the Alans would have provided hunting mastiffs as well as horses, their renowned Alaunts. The governors of Milan were once commended 'because... there have sprung up in our region noble Destriers (the war horses of medieval knights) which are held in high estimation. They also reared Alanian dogs of high stature and wonderful courage.' Chaucer did of course refer to 'Alauns' as big as steers; the type was evidently acknowledged here then.

As the cavalry for the Roman legions, the Alans have left their mark in Britain. The Avon in Hampshire was once called the Alaun, as was the Alne in Northumberland. Allaway in Scotland comes from this source too. In his very informative The Master of Game of 1410, the renowned hunter Gaston de Foix's words on French dogs are reworked by Edward, second Duke of York. He describes the Alaunt as a hound 'better shaped and stronger for to do harm than any other beast'; he made a distinction between mastiffs and Alaunts. He regarded the latter as seizing dogs, the former as big running mastiffs, for use in the chase. De Foix was the greatest hunter of his time, maintaining a kennel of over a thousand sporting dogs. He would not have blurred mastiffs with Alaunts, he used them in different ways. They had different functions.

In England, the name 'mastiff' wasn't in common use until quite a late date, the end of the 18th century; Osbaldiston, in his famous dictionary, utilises the long-established word of Saxon origin 'bandogge'. Scholars are not always reliable sources of information on breeds or types of dog. Sherwood, in his dictionary, defines a mastiff as an Alan. Cotgrave, in his dictionary, records: 'Allan: kinde of big, strong, thicke-headed, and short-snowted dog; the brood whereof came first out of Albania (old Epirus)'. He is confusing the more recent state of Albania with the ancient country also called Albania, near the Caspian Sea. This latter region is the part of the world where the nomadic Alans originated. But Cotgrave's confusion has not stopped subsequent dog breed researchers from firmly linking Alaunts with the Molossian dog from ancient Epirus, adding further confusion.

Even worse, Jesse, in his *Researches into the History of the British Dog* of 1866, like Turbervile before him, presents The Master of Game's descriptions as referring to British dogs, whereas they referred to French ones. But even more misleading to mastiff researchers is Markham's work in 1616; he tendentiously mistranslated Gratius's Cynegeticon to state that the Romans found 'mastiffs' on reaching the shores of Britain. As the distinguished American historian Jan Libourel has helpfully pointed out, what Gratius actually wrote was: 'If you want a good hound, a trip to Britain would almost be worth it.

The British dogs may not look much, but for bravery in combat even the famous Molossus does not surpass them.' The word mastiff was never used in this much misused quote.

The recklessly brave dogs which closed with the boar in the medieaval hunt were boar lurchers in today's phraseology. The broad-mouthed dogs which survive, the once coarsely bred mastiff-types developed by show-men into distinct breeds and now being ruined in today's show rings, have a remarkable heritage and deserve all the respect we can afford them.

Medieval hunt – bandogges in foreground.

The Albanian Wolfhound. (Charwynne Dog Features)

Irish Greyhound or Wolf-dog, 1850.

BELOW: **Wolves and their opponents.**
(from Goldsmith's *An History of the Earth and Animated Nature* 1774)

THE WOLF LURCHER

Huge shaggy-coated hunting dogs were used by the Celts in their central European homeland in the 8th century BC and these accompanied them on their migrations to Britain, Ireland and Northern Spain from the 5th to the 1st century BC. In his *Gentleman's Recreation* of 1675, Nicholas Cox wrote: 'Although we have no wolves in England at the present, yet it is certain that heretofore we had routs of them, as they have to this very day in Ireland; and in that country are bred a race of Greyhounds which are commonly called wolfdogs, which are strong, fleet and bear a natural enmity to the wolf. Now in these Greyhounds of that nation there is an incredible force and boldness...'

Behind the Irish Wolfhound there are at least three distinct types: Just over one hundred years ago, Fitzinger identified '...The Irish Greyhound, next to the Indian and Russian Greyhound, is the largest specimen of the Greyhound type, combining the speed of the Greyhound with the size of the Mastiff. The second type is the Irish coursing dog, a cross between the Irish Greyhound and the Mastiff or bandogge. He is shorter in the neck, with a coarser skull, broader chest and heavily flewed lips'. The third variety he described as a cross between the Irish Greyhound and the shepherd dog, being low on the leg and having a shaggy coat. The latter sounds like a shepherd's mastiff or native flock guardian, a bigger version of the Irish Beardie or hirsel.

Lord Altamont wrote to the Linnaean Society in 1800 to state that: 'There were formerly in Ireland two kinds of wolfdogs – the Greyhound and the Mastiff. Till within these two years I was possessed of both kinds, perfectly distinct, and easily known from each other. The heads were not so sharp in the latter as the former; but there seemed a great similarity in temper and disposition, both being harmless and indolent.' He stated that the painting held by the Society was of the mastiff wolfdog; it was 28 inches at the shoulder.

The Countess of Blessington in Ireland was presented with a giant Suliot Dog by the King of Naples. Lady Blessington was one of the Powers of Kilfane, who at one time were the only people who patronised the Irish Wolfhound. Suliot Dogs came from Epirus in Greece, location of the Molossian people, and were giant hounds, used as outpost sentries in the Austrian Army and as 'parade dogs' or mascots of German regiments. They were used to give added stature to German boarhounds (the hunting dogs being nearer to 26 inches at the shoulder than the 30 inches minimum of today's Great Danes). Lady Blessington's Suliot Dog is likely to have been used as a sire at Kilfane.

The Irish Wolfhound was all but lost to us in the latter half of the 19th century. Then, in 1863, an Englishman, Captain George Augustus Graham, a Deerhound breeder, noted that some of his stock threw back to the larger type of Irish Wolfhound. He obtained dogs of the Kilfane and Ballytobin strains, the only suitable blood available in Ireland at that time. He then inter-bred these with Glengarry Deerhounds, which had Irish Wolfhound blood in their own ancestry. In due course he produced and then stabilised the type of Irish Wolfhound which he believed to be historically correct. Outcrossing continued, with Capt Graham using the blood of a 'great dog of Tibet'; then, between 1885 and 1900, seven Great Dane crosses were conducted, and Borzoi blood used several times in the 1890s. This is of course how all hunting dogs were once bred, good dog to good dog, irrespective of breed titles. Closed gene pools are a modern phenomenon.

The Indian wolf has been hunted using similarly shaggy-coated hounds, like the Banjara or Vanjari, 28 inches high and grey mottled, and the 30 inch Rampur Hound, the smoother-coated Shikari dog of Kumaon, the Great Dane-like Sindh Hound, the beautiful ivory-coated Rajapalayam and the Dobermann-shaped Patti of Tamilnad. Such types disappear when the threat from wolves recedes but their value to man was considerable. Our contemporary affection for the wolf would not have been shared by those living in remote villages in India or a number of European countries in the middle ages. Wolves, operating in packs, threatened livestock and sought human prey when desperate for food. Powerful dogs of the flock guarding type were needed to protect livestock and strong-headed very fast hounds were needed to course them. Hunting wolves for sport may not appeal to 21st century sympathies, but that should not lessen our admiration for wolfhounds, their bravery and athleticism in the hunt, when wolf numbers required checking.

In medieaval times, there were laws under which some court fines were assessed in terms of wolves' tongues. At one time, the yearly tax in Wales was established at 300 wolves' heads. France was one country particularly populated by wolves; as early as 1467, Louis XI created a special wolf-hunting office, whose top member was appointed from the highest families in the land. In the French province of Gevaudan in the 1760s one wolf is alleged to have killed more than fifty people, the majority women and children. At the end of the French revolution in 1797, 40 people were killed by wolves, tens of thousands of sheep, goats and horses slaughtered by them, and, in some remote districts, not a single watchdog left alive. The dense forests led to the French mainly hunting them with packs of scent hounds rather than coursing them with faster hounds.

But the hound hunting the wolf using speed was the Borzoi, a wolf lurcher in many ways, with so many varieties across a huge country. The graceful athletic build of the Russian Wolfhound has long drawn widespread admiration: Charles Darwin described them as an 'embodiment of symmetry and beauty'. Undoubtedly the attractive silky coat of the modern pedigree Borzoi enhances its physical appearance. But as with the Saluki and the Ibizan hound, of this type of swift hound, there were varieties of coat in the Borzoi too. *The Hunter's Calendar and Reference Book*, published in Moscow in 1892, divided the Borzoi into four groups. First,

Russian or Psovoy Borzoi, more or less long-coated; second, Asiatic, with pendant ears; third, Hortoy, smooth-coated; fourth, the Brudastoy, stiff-coated or wire-haired. But whether the hounds were sleek or bristle-haired, wolf coursing in Russia before the Revolution was what fox-hunting was to Britain and par force hunting was to France.

As Leo Tolstoi recorded in *War and Peace*: 'Fifty-four coursing hounds were taken with six mounted horsemen and keepers of hounds. Apart from the Master and his guests, another eight huntsmen took part, with more than forty hounds. In the end, there were one hundred and thirty hounds and twenty horsemen in the field.' Tsar Peter II kept a pack consisting of 200 coursing hounds and over 420 Greyhounds. Prince Somzonov of Smolensk had 1,000 hounds at his hunting box, calling himself Russia's Prime Huntsman. Better known was the hunt with the Perchino hounds near Tula on the river Upa, where Archduke Nicolai Nikolsevich established a hunting box in 1887 and hunted two packs of 120 par force hounds, 120 to 150 Borzoi and 15 English Greyhounds. To ensure sufficient hardiness for winter wolf hunts, both horses and hounds were kept in unheated stables or kennels.

Usually 20 leashes of Borzois were taken to a hunt, each consisting of two males and a bitch. The hunting season was summer coursing (June to early August) on hare or fox, then summer training for Borzois in August. This consisted of 20 kilometres walking or trotting with the hunt horses, followed by advanced training on captive wolves in early September, then the wolf-coursing season from mid-September to the end of October. Hunting from sledges sometimes took place from October, with mounted beaters putting up the wolves, which were often fed to keep them in the hunting grounds. In the Perchino game reserve, between 1887 and 1913, 681 wolves were killed, as well as 743 foxes, 4,630 brown hares and 4,026 white hares; Borzois obtaining the bulk of this bag.

Whatever the rights and wrongs of hunting on such a scale, the robustness, fitness and stamina of the hounds must have been remarkable. Coursing with Borzois in Tsarist Russia called for a high

Irish Wolfhound Ch Ballyshannon, bred by the Rev C H Hildebrand. Soundly constructed – as all huge dogs must be. Depicted in 1925.

Suliot Dog of Countess Blessington.

Wolf lurchers at work. (Charwynne Dog Features)

standard of horsemanship and superbly trained hounds. Each mounted handler rode with his three hounds on long leashes, slipping the hounds whenever a wolf was either put up by the extended line of mounted beaters or flushed out of the woods by scent hounds of the Gontchaja type. Many of us would find it difficult enough to control three Borzois on short leashes whilst dismounted! The Borzoi is still important for the Russian fur trade, for they catch foxes without mauling them and ruining their pelts. This also avoids the crueller use of iron spring traps.

Against that background, it is surely important for us to respect past function, which bequeathed us the wolfhound breeds, and breed to reflect that heritage. In Albania, well into the 20th century, cross-bred dogs to combat wolves were still found vital in remote areas. Wolves can easily kill dogs, especially when fighting for their own lives; the big shaggy-coated recklessly determined coarsely bred dogs used on wolf in Northern Europe for centuries, often a blend of shepherd's mastiff and hound, wolf lurchers in fact, deserve our recognition for their service and, all too often, self-sacrifice.

Wolf-lurchers at work.
(Charwynne Dog Features)

CHAPTER 3

SOURCES OF SPEED

The amazing extension of the Greyhound in full gallop.

Racing Greyhound: built for speed.
(Courtesy of the magazine *The Greyhound*) (Charwynne Dog Features)

Borzoi at speed.
At a recent Afghan Hound racing meet, a number of breeds were raced over set distances. Over 660 metres, the fastest Greyhound cross was Billy Ray Leonard in 45.49, fastest Saluki Jade Gardiner did 53.38, fastest lurcher was Dexter Gardiner at 51.90. Over 260 metres, the fastest lurcher was Alfie Gardiner at 26.03. It is important to keep in mind however that in lurchers, sagacity comes before speed.

HUNTING BY SPEED

'Graceful as the swallow's flight,
Light as swallow, winged one,
Swift as driven hurricane -
Double-sinewed stretch and spring,
Muffled thud of flying feet...'

Those words of Julian Grenfell, in his poem *The Black Greyhound*, one hundred years ago, convey at once the speed, grace and power of the sighthound breeds. Many of these breeds are glamorous, like the Afghan Hound, physically beautiful, like the Saluki, aristocratic, like the Borzoi, and seemingly gentle-natured, like the Deerhound. But they were designed and then bred to hunt, not just to attend fashion models on location for photo shoots, which often seems to be a favoured employment for them in recent times. I have no criticism of that but I am concerned that such attractive breeds can end up being valued only for their looks and their spiritual needs overlooked. Their instinct to chase and catch other animals too needs to be acknowledged. These are dogs designed more for a cat-chase than a catwalk!

Sighthound as a descriptive noun for a function is misleading; all dogs hunt by sight even when following a scent. The sighthounds hunt by speed, they succeed because of their speed. Agility matters hugely in the chase, for all quarry can run! Stamina has to accompany speed and agility too. In the Middle East I have watched two Salukis race out of sight over ground which would have broken some dogs' legs and over a distance which would have taken the pace out of many hounds. I was not surprised when a lurcher breeder once told me that the greatest benefit from the blood of the Saluki came in the feet. The Afghan Hound also needs remarkable feet to cope with the terrain in its native country. We may not want our Afghans and Salukis to sprint over rocks or our Borzois to hunt wolves, but they came to us as breeds developed for a function and with an anatomy which allowed them to perform that function. We ignore that original function and we imperil the breed.

With that in mind it was worrying to read recent show critiques on the Afghan Hound. At Crufts in 1999, the judge remarked: '...I do feel attention must be concentrated on the shoulder conformation, the true angle of well laid back shoulders, plus a good length of upper arm, bringing the forelegs well under the body, thus giving good forward movement and return, *this is sadly missing in most Afghans*.' Similar comments were made by the LKA judge that year: '...front assemblies i.e. correct angulation in upper arm and shoulder, and in balance with each other, ought to be watched.' The judge at the Southern Afghan Club championship show stated: '...I was somewhat taken aback by the chests and ribbing of some of the dogs...', lamenting the short rib cages. Afghan Hounds with these faults would not last five minutes in the hunting grounds of their native country. Respecting a breed's function is crucial in breeding typical dogs.

We have to be extraordinarily careful that in the pursuit of show ring success we do not end up destroying the key elements in these beautiful *functional* breeds. A sighthound needs lung and heart room in abundance; it must have great forward extension, facilitated by sound shoulders. Straight upper arms are creeping into so many sporting breeds these days and it is introducing quite untypical and most undesirable movement. Cynics may say that Afghans are judged mainly on their coats nowadays and I've heard it said that American show breeders want every breed to look like the Irish Setter in profile. But real lovers of any breed surely value type and their breed's characteristics. I cannot see the logic of admiring a foreign breed and then 'trying to make a new version', as the Afghan Hound judge put it.

The importance of sound shoulders can never be stressed enough in any hound breed. Yet judges constantly comment on deficiencies in this area. The judge of Whippet dogs at Crufts 2000 wrote: 'Shoulder angulation still requires attention, there were too many with short upper arms and incorrect layback of the shoulder blades'. A hound built for speed, whether a Spanish Galgo, a Hungarian Agar, a Tasy or a Taigon from Mid-Asia, a Moroccan Sloughi or an Azawakh from Mali, *must* have the anatomical attributes which provide sprinting power. Some foreign sighthound breeds look different now from the original imports; the Afghan Hound certainly has more coat and the Borzoi can feature a markedly convex back as opposed to the more or less level topline of the early hounds.

In *The Hunter's Calendar and Reference Book* published in Moscow in 1892, the Borzoi is divided into four groups: Old Russian or Psovoy/ Gustopsovoy Borzoi, with the longer coat, Asiatic, with pendant ears, Hortoy, smooth-coated, and Brudastoy, stiff or wire-haired. At the Crystal Palace Show in the 1890s a man called Zambaco exhibited a Circassian Orloff Wolfhound called Domovoy, 32½ inches at the shoulder and wolf-coloured. It was described as being longer-legged than the Siberian hound, with a flat, close-lying coat rather than a wavy one. At the Botanic Gardens Show of 1903, a Circassian Harehound, 20½ inches at the shoulder and silky-haired, was exhibited. She had particularly large feet and was said to turn tighter than a Greyhound.

Circassia, now part of the Karachayevo-Cherkess region of Russia, was once under Turkish rule, being north of the Caucasus near the Black Sea. Not surprisingly, many regions featured their own sighthound variety, the hounds' capability as pot-fillers being valued. The Polish Greyhound, Chart Polski, from further north is exhibited at the World Shows but the Albanian Wolfhound, from the Balkans, has not emerged as a distinct breed. All these hounds, wherever they come from, display the classic sighthound phenotype: tucked-up belly, long narrow head, long straight muscular legs, arched loin, ribs carried well back, long neck, sloping shoulders, level topline, croup falling away to allow great forward extension from the powerful hindlegs, mobile ears and a long tail.

This sighthound mould developed from function and a show judge who doesn't punish upright shoulders and short upper arms is doing the sighthound breeds a considerable disservice. Movement of course reveals such faults, a well-constructed sighthound should 'daisy-clip' with spring in its step and a minimal uplift of feet. This effortlessness when moving is a prized sighthound asset and directly related to correct construction. The Afghan Hound has a higher front foot action, perhaps from a greater length of upper arm and claimed to originate from having to negotiate rocky terrain in its native country. Yet there is no appreciable difference in movement between the desert or plains type and that from the foothills.

It is so pleasing to know that Afghan Hound (and Saluki) racing is conducted in Britain; what a release for the hounds! Less pleasing is the knowledge that the best Afghan Hound racer, Fox Ellis, which won the national individual championship a record five successive times, was never used at stud. A litter sister became a champion but for Fox Ellis not to be used at stud tells you more about breeders seeking show-winner blood ahead of proven construction than I ever could. The sighthound breeds only survived to enter the show arenas because of their ability to race. In this connection it was sad when in refusing registration to fine Syrian Salukis one enthusiast wished to import the Kennel Club gave the comment: 'It would be difficult to believe that breeding patterns within desert tribes would be as

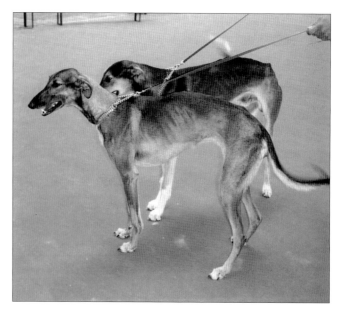

Chart Polski: Polish Sighthounds.
(Charwynne Dog Features)

LEFT: **The Whippet is very much a hunting dog.**

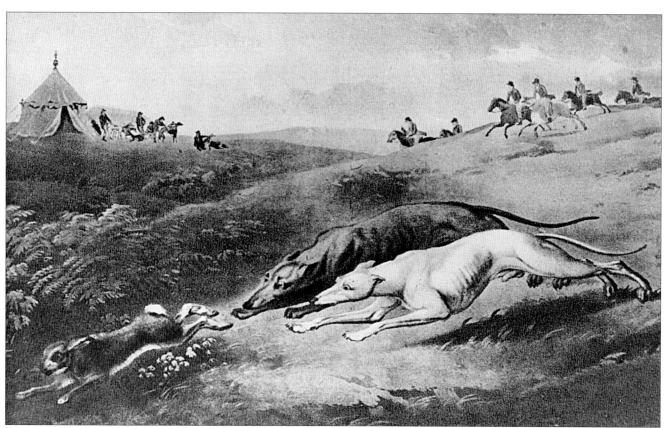

Coursing (Coloured aquatint after Philip Reinagle by Nichols and Black, 1815). (Charwynne Dog Features)

Lord Lurgan's Master McGrath (by Dervock ex Lady Sarah) winner of the Waterloo Cup 1868, 1869, 1871.

Pentonville, winner of the Wateloo Cup in 1925. A beautifully symmetrical dog. Wherever man introduces exaggeration nature finds a weakness.

Hard-shouldered dogs of old: Messrs Fawcett's Waterloo Cup winners: all reared on Cumberland Fells.
(Charwynne Dog Features)

Cushey Job, winner of The Waterloo Cup in 1924. A winning Greyhound with powerful hindquarters.

BELOW: **Edmund Bristowe:** *Greyhounds*, **the property of W Adams.**
(Charwynne Dog Features)

No, not a Greyhound but a Magyar Agar.
(Charwynne Dog Features)

strictly controlled as those under the aegis of the Kennel Club.'

This needlessly pompous statement reflects badly on the KC, whose 'strictly controlled breeding patterns' are based solely on breeder honesty. Arabian breeding patterns are decided entirely by performance. Whose sighthounds would you prefer? An infusion of genes from sighthounds judged wholly on performance would have done the breed of Saluki in Britain so much good. Closed gene pools so often indicate closed minds too.

Some historians believe that the sighthounds in Eastern Arabia came from Asia originally. Studies on the blood of the Azawakh and the Sloughi showed that both have an additional allele on the glucose phosphate isomerase gene locus not found in other sighthounds and dogs but present in the coyote, fox and jackal. These two African breeds showed the greatest genetic distance from the other dogs in this study. This suggests a different historical development. Wherever any sighthound breed comes from and whatever its coat length, we should respect their heritage, perpetuate them as honourably as Bedouins do and 'control' their breeding just as strictly as the latter do. Is any sighthound *not* built for speed really a sighthound at all? A lurcher with sighthound conformation might hunt well, but for sheer speed the sighthound build will always prevail.

GREYHOUNDS OF 1866: CANINE ATHLETES.
Of a Greyhound's liveweight, roughly 57% is accounted for by muscle. This compares with around 40% for most mammals. During exercise, a Greyhound can increase its packed (blood) cell volume by between 60 and 70%, and increase its heart beat from below 100 to over 300 per minute; this allows a much more effective blood flow to its muscles than is the case in most other breeds. The Greyhound's thigh muscles are far better developed than in most other breeds, facilitating pace.

THE GREYHOUND

'The Greyhound, the great Hound, the graceful of limb,
Rough fellow, tall fellow, swift fellow and slim;
Set them round o'er the earth, let them sail o'er the sea,
They will light on none other more ancient than he.'

Those words commendably celebrate the sheer antiquity of the Greyhound but surprisingly pay less attention to the reason for that long history: the dog's quite remarkable speed. Dogs can achieve astounding speeds when serving man. A top sled-dog team can race through snow-clad woods at speeds up to 3.2 minutes a mile – for several days! Blue Cap, the famous Foxhound, is alleged to have covered four miles of Newmarket racecourse in just over eight minutes, in a renowned match race in 1762. That is roughly the speed of a Derby winner at Epsom. But over the sprints there is nothing to match a Greyhound.

A Greyhound can cover 5/16ths of a mile in 30 seconds. In each decade the feats are repeated: in 1932, Ataxy did 525 yards in 29.56 seconds, and, in 1936, 725 yards in 41.69 seconds. In 1971, Dolores Rocket did the 525 yard course in 28.52 seconds. In 1944, Ballyhennessy Seal set what was then a new world record for 500 yards in 27.64 seconds. The legendary Mick the Miller did the 600 yards in 34.01 seconds in 1930. He was spoken of as combining 'tranquillity with trackcraft'. In other words he never wasted energy nervously and used the circuit cleverly. When he died he was found to have a heart weighing 1½ oz above the normal for a Greyhound of his size.

Of course hounds with a comparable build can also achieve great speed; a 32lb Whippet was once recorded as covering 150 yards in 8.6 seconds. This build is a superb combination of bone and muscle, a unique balance between size/weight and strength

and quite remarkable coordination between fore and hindlimbs. The Greyhound sprints in a series of leaps rather than running in a strict sense. It is what is termed a 'double-flight' runner, where the feet are all off the ground at the same moment. This is unlike a 'single-flight' animal like the horse which, when racing, nearly always has at least one foot on the ground.

The Greyhound's leaping gait is rooted in quite exceptional extension, especially forward with the hind legs, but also rearwards with the front legs. Anatomically, the most vital elements in such a dog are the shoulders, and their placement, and the pelvic slope, which determines the forward extension of the all-important hindlimbs. That's where the power comes from. It always saddens me to see a sighthound in the show ring displaying upright shoulders and short upper arms, together with a lack of pelvic slope. It is even sadder when such an exhibit is placed by an ignorant judge! I see these faults especially in Afghan Hounds, but also in Salukis, Borzois and Whippets, as well as in lurchers at country shows.

But I do see more correctly constructed 'Greyhound-Lurchers' than I do show Greyhounds. This is a comment rather than a criticism, because I see many more of the former than the latter. It is worrying however to see a lack of muscle on show Greyhounds and at times a slab-sidedness which affects type as well as function. Sporting breeds must be judged in any ring on their ability to carry out their specific historic function, if not then there is really little point in breeding them. Breed points have no value if a breed loses its precious ability to work. Breeds came to us from a function; the essential thread running through a breed, its breed clubs and its fanciers, is surely that of keeping faith with its functional design.

There is a need too to respect the noble heritage of the Greyhound, this breed is so much more than a 'grey hound'. As with far too many breed titles, with the Tibetan breeds of dog standing out as classic examples, that of the Greyhound is misleading. The inclusion of the letter 'Y' in the Greyhound's breed name gives an immediate hint that this breed earned its title from being a hound distinctly grey. The importance of this mis-spelling lies in the fact that gre-hund meant a 'noble, great, choice or prize-hound'. Three notable authorities: Jesse, Dalziel and Baillie-Grohman, all agree on this; their word is good enough for me. A Welsh proverb stated that a gentleman might be known, and judged, 'by his hawk, his horse and his Greyhound'. By a law of Canute, a Greyhound was not to be kept by any person inferior to a gentleman. The Greyhound was clearly the companion of noblemen and deserves the more distinctive title of Grehund or noble hound. Confusingly, in the Middle Ages, the word Grey-hound was used loosely to refer to such diverse types as the Irish Wolfhound, the Scottish Deerhound and the dainty diminutive Italian Greyhound. Such dogs were the close companions of men involved in war and travel to far-off countries. It is therefore most unwise to link the contemporary breed of Grey-hound with portraits of such men. Caius, in 1576, made extensive reference to the Greyhound, by name, calling it in Latin: *Leporarius*, after its hare-hunting employment. He made quite *separate* reference to the gazehound, quite clearly regarding the latter as a par force hound, not a sighthound. The par force hounds made the hunt into a steeplechase, hunting by sight when their prey was literally within sight, only reverting to scent when hunting in wooded or close country, or on losing sight of their quarry. A gazehound is not a sighthound by another name.

Greyhound researchers usually make much of an early reference to the breed in England by Dame Berners in her *Boke of St Albans*. But her memorable description 'Heded like a snake, and necked like a drake. Foted like a cat. Tayled like a Rat' is a clear plagiarism of Gace de la Buigne, written some time previously and not in England. The Ancient Greeks prized their sighthounds, Arrian writing: '...the fast running Celtic hounds are called vertragi in the Celtic

language... these have their name from their speed... the best bred of them are a fine sight.' The Italian for a Greyhound is veltro, veltre in Old French, from the Celtic word guilter. The Spanish for a Greyhound is galgo, derived from gallicu, a word meaning Gaullish hound.

Today the Galgo is the breed of Spanish Grey-hound, just as the Chart Polski is the Polish one and the Magyar Agar the Hungarian version. At a distance all could be confused with a smooth Saluki, a Sloughi or an Azawakh, such is the universal silhouette of a smooth-haired sighthound. (Although the Galgo can feature the rough coat too.) No doubt, the Shilluk Greyhound from the plains of the White Nile in southern Sudan displays the same characteristic phenotype too. In India, there are the Vaghari and Pashmi hounds, the Rajapalayam and Rampur dogs, the Poligar and the Chippiparai dogs, all with clear smooth-haired sighthound anatomies along what we would term Greyhound lines. To run fast a dog needs long legs, a long body, great muscular development but not too much weight.

The weight of successful coursing Greyhounds is worth a glance. The renowned Master M'Grath was around 53lb, Bit of Fashion was 54lb, Golden Seal, Staff Officer, Guards Brigade, White Collar and Fitz Fife were each around 65lb but Shortcoming only 49lb. Our show Greyhound has no stipulation regarding weight but its ideal height, for a male dog, is desired at 28 to 30 inches. A Deerhound dog of 30 inches at the withers would weigh around 100lb. Does a Greyhound need to be 30 inches high and approaching a hundredweight? Why does a show Greyhound need to be twice the weight of a successful coursing Greyhound? The American KC standard sets the Greyhound's weight at 65 to 70lb for a dog and 60 to 65lb for a bitch.

The racing Greyhound community is not short of handsome dogs, despite the over-riding priority given to performance. I do have concerns about two aspects of this industry: the number of dogs abandoned to the rescue system and the penalties to so many dogs of bend racing. Hard surfaces and heavier dogs combine to increase the danger of serious injuries to Greyhounds when racing round bends at

Mr R N Stoller's Sylph and Saracen by Such a Mark-Game 'un. Constructed to run fast.
Greyhounds Mannd Earl 1900
(Charwynne Dog Features)

GREYHOUNDS AT CRUFTS
This depicts Champion Treetops Golden Falcon, the Best in Show at Crufts in 1956. In 1928, the Greyhound Primly Sceptre won Best in Show at Crufts, the first to win the new award. Increasing numbers of racing-bred Greyhounds are being entered for Crufts, perpetuating a long tradition. In 1929, the entry was 252 from 187 Greyhounds, of which only 17 were show-bred, the coursing entry prevailing. Earnest Goitre's bundle 70lb dog, Endless Gossip, is the most famous racing Greyhound to appear at Crufts; he won the 1952 Greyhound Derby and performed well in the 1953 Waterloo Cup. At Crufts 2009, in the racing/coursing entry, there was a striking black bitch Lupine Lenin Lacers Louses, which perfectly exemplified the correct conformation for the breed.

Coursing scene (1850).

Greyhounds: Mr W Long's 'David' and Mr C Randell's 'Riot'. 19th century course.

ABOVE: **A Greyhound needs great muscular development.**

Major, the winner of the 1000 Guineas challenge on Epsom Downs. (from *Sportsman's Cabinet*, 1803)

tracks. Statistics show that over the years, by the time the Greyhound Derby final is run each year, at least 40 of the entries will have sustained injury (Sweeney, 1980). I suspect that the heavier dogs receive the highest injury rate. Greyhounds have very vulnerable feet and legs, especially over sun-baked or frozen going. Expecting them to cope with unyielding ground *and* considerable weight is not wise.

On the credit side, the Greyhound seems resistant to the worrying increase in cranial cruciate ligament rupture in dogs. A study of 821 cases of this disorder found that 77 were Rottweilers but not one a racing Greyhound. The straighter stifle joint of the Rottweiler may play a part in this tendency but it is encouraging to note the greater robustness of the Greyhound's hindlimbs. The Greyhound is less liable to hip dysplasia than any other breed. On the debit side is the worrying sensitivity of the Greyhound to anaesthetic, due to its lack of body fat. It is scarcely surprising for a breed capable of such speed to suffer more injuries in the chase; injuries creating a need for the administration of anaesthetics before treatment do however cause concern in the breed.

It is significant that in lure-racing in Canada over the 1970s and 80s the most successful hounds were the 'half-and-halfs', i.e. show–track crosses. They were found to have greater endurance and recuperative powers. Track dogs possess greater speed but are not bred to run several races in quick succession. Thirty years ago, in the United States, the Coursing Greyhound of the Year was the American show champion Strider; he was a show–track cross. This would be unthinkable here in the current thinking, more's the pity. Most racing Greyhounds weigh between 64 and 77lb for dogs and 45 and 55lb for bitches. In America and Ireland the weights can be higher. But I know of no successful racing or coursing Greyhound of around 100lb, the weight of some of our show dogs.

The Greyhound is the supreme canine athlete. Our Greyhounds have been exported all over the world because of their athletic excellence. It could be argued that the Greyhound represents the major source of quality in our lurchers; certainly their speed is a major source of success in lurcher work.

VARIETIES OF THE MODERN GREYHOUND

'The Newmarket Greyhound. This variety stands at the head of the list as the probable root of all our modern subdivisions... the Greyhounds running there, being eagerly sought after throughout the length and breadth of the land... superior to all others... the most racing-like dog... yet possessed of as much stoutness as possible, in combination with great speed.

The Lancashire Greyhound... must be large and strong... possessed of tact and cleverness... I am inclined to think that the Lancashire has the superiority in persistence.

The Yorkshire Greyhound is characterised by speed as great as that of Newmarket or Lancashire, coupled with a degree of cleverness rarely seen elsewhere.

The Wiltshire Greyhound was formerly bred exclusively for the extraordinary hares which are generally met with there... These hares are generally fast, but they also have the power of throwing out even the best worker in a style quite different to the Lancashire and Yorkshire variety. Hence, the Wiltshire dog has been bred especially strong and stout-hearted...'

John Henry Walsh, *The Pursuit of Wild Animals for Sport*, 1856

Yellow Printer, the fastest Irish Greyhound Derby winner when he won in 1968. Note the extraordinary extension required to attain this reach.

Local Interprize, winner in 1948 of three classic events, the Cesarewitch, the Gold Collar and the Scurry Gold Cup. Note the long rib cage and well let-down hocks on this dog

LEFT: 'Fullerton', winner of the Waterloo Cup in 1890–1–2 divided in 1889. Note the remarkable length fron haunch to hock.

BELOW LEFT: Monday's News, winner of the English Greyhound Derby 1946 and the Pall Mall 1947. Note the depth of chest on this outstanding dog.

BELOW: Thoughtful Beauty, winner of the Waterloo Cup in 1895. Note the powerful loin on this outstanding dog.

The Greyhound – not a Gaze Hound but very much a Sight Hound.

RIGHT: **Greyhounds – designed to run – very fast!**

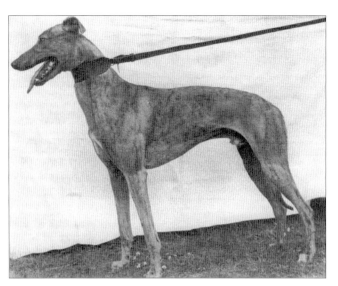

Smartly Fergus, one-time holder of the 600 yds record at Celtic Park and the 525 yds record at Shelbourne Park. Note the amount of ground covered by this dog – just standing.

Outside blood can revitalise – An Australian cross, 1928. Mrs B J Fuller, wife of Captain B J Fuller, is introducing fresh blood into the Greyhound breed of England and Ireland by crossing with imported Australian Greyhounds. Once Australia was imported by Mrs Oscar Asche, and 'Lady Pangbourne' and 'Ballyshannon, amongst others, are descended from a cross with that Australian matron.

MICK THE MILLER'S OWNER
Mrs A H Kempton with some of her famous dogs bred out of Loftwood Misery, the winner of about £10,000 on racing tracks and a great popular favourite. Mick goes back to the Duke of Leeds' stock.

The Saluki: beauty combined with function. (D Copperthwaite)

Saluki lurcher. (Charwynne Dog Features)

Sloughi. (Charwynne Dog Features)

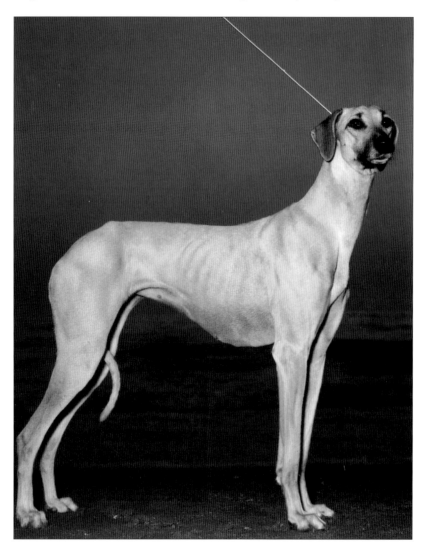

THE SALUKI

'There are two major types of sighthound depicted in Egyptian art. The first is the slender, erect-eared, curly-tailed canine commonly referred to in scholarly and literary works as a tesem...A second type of sighthound pictured in Egyptian art has a shorter, heavier muzzle than the tesem, is lop-eared and has a curved or sabre tail. This type of dog is commonly referred to in the modern literature as a Saluki...That Saluki-type dogs often appear taller and more graceful than the tesem suggests they are a more refined sighthound, clearly adapted for speed.'

Douglas Brewer, Terence Clark & Adrian Phillips *Dogs in Antiquity*, Aris & Phillips, 2001

What does the Saluki bring to the lurcher table? Good feet, great stamina, remarkable single-mindedness? Or are they just sighthounds which prefer to chase their prey rather than actually catch it? If you wish to counterbalance some of the Saluki's qualities with better traits in other blood, which 'other blood' is best? Good feet, great stamina and single-mindedness are fine but do they alone catch the quarry?

There is nothing unique to Britain in the use by hunters of Saluki-cross sheepdogs as versatile hunting dogs, which use speed, scent and stamina to catch their quarry. In Iraq, the 'luqi' or Saluki crossed with a local sheepdog has long been used as a 'thinking' sighthound. The quarry would be gazelle, fox or hare; the ground mostly rocky but very muddy in the rainy season and the 'going' extremely testing, especially to the feet. The 'luqi' is prized for its superior nose, in conditions where scenting is surprisingly difficult. Perhaps too this sheepdog blood made the 'luqi' more biddable, something many lurcher men here seek in their Saluki-cross dogs. The Kurds produced the khilasi, a cross between their Saluqi and a Kurdish sheepdog, to improve scenting ability and response to training. In south Syria, the Arabs bred the zaghuri, allegedly from an outcross to a zeiger, Old High German for a pointer, said to have been introduced by the Crusaders, to enhance scenting power.

I have known men famed for their skill at training hunting dogs of all kinds regularly reduced to the hair-tearing stage when faced with an independently minded Saluki. Is it perversity, wilfulness, lack of concentration, periodic deafness or just straightforward stubbornness which makes this breed so trying? My abiding memory of hare-coursing in Jordan is of the need for a jeep with a well-filled tank and powerful binoculars, not to find the game, but to recover the hounds! But for the patient, the stoical and the long-suffering, the rewards, in the end, of seeing a once-exasperating Saluki mature into a good reliable hunting dog are manifold. (Perhaps understood best, in different fields, by Basset Hound and Clumber Spaniel owners!) But what a sight a Saluki is – at full stretch; they seem to fly across ground which a human being couldn't jog over.

The advice I received from the bedouin about the criteria for a sighthound to run fast for extended periods over difficult terrain boils down to just two points: girth of chest and girth of loin. Heart and lung room and power of propulsion would be another way of putting it. The users of gazelle hounds in the desert looked for, in say a 26 inch hound, a girth of chest of 26 to 31 inches and a girth of loin from 18 to 24 inches. The bedouin don't bother with breed descriptions Kennel Club-style, with flowery accounts of anatomical beauty. From al-Mutawakkili, writing in the 9th century, we can however learn that a long body with a short back, powerful loins, deep chest, fleshy shoulders and powerful flanks were valued by the hunters of those times.

Lurcher men were slow to appreciate the value of

Saluki blood for some years. Even now however show-bred Salukis with shelly bodies and few hunting instincts are being utilised by lurcher breeders in the forlorn hope that some good Saluki features will be inherited in their breeding programmes. I'm surprised that some enterprising soul hasn't imported *real* hunting Salukis from the Middle East, hounds with a known field performance. Lurcher men would be the first to admit however that the Salukis deployed to the field by the admirable Saluki Coursing Club are fine hounds. 'Amena Viceroy of Anasazi' won the Scottish thirty-two dog, three day stake three years in succession, the only hound to achieve this in the thirty years of the event. Salukis like this deserve all the praise we can muster.

But for those who seek pedigree status and need registration for their imported stock, the Kennel Club has not been particularly cooperative. Sir Terence Clark KBE CMG CVO, once our ambassador in Oman and a keen coursing man, who knows and appreciates hunting Salukis, has raised this issue with the KC. Not a show-ring fancier, Sir Terence was anxious that Saluki breeders here should benefit from the fine hunting stock, often crop-eared and lacking the breed points of the KC pedigree Saluki, available in countries like Iraq. But they could not be registered by those who would wish to do so.

Incidentally in replying to Sir Terence's letter, the then secretary of the Kennel Club, General Sinnatt, wrote: '...it would be difficult to believe that breeding patterns within desert tribes would be as strictly controlled as those under the aegis of the Kennel Club'. This, despite the fact that every Saluki in Britain originated from the 'breeding patterns within desert tribes' referred to by the chief executive of the KC.

The Saluki judge at Crufts 2007 recorded: 'I wondered where the breed is heading...Hindquarters were a particular worry with lack of length and substance to upper thighs.' The KC tells us that these are 'the best of the very best': what must the non-

qualifiers be like! At the Saluki or Gazelle Club show of 2006, the judge reported: 'I was shocked at how poorly many dogs move.' At two other shows that year comments ranged from a lack of quality in depth and lack of forward reach to plaiting and close movement behind. The Arabs could send some improving blood, if only our KC would let them!

The famed areas for the best Salukis as hunting dogs have long been the Wadi Sirhan in Syria and Rutba on the Jordan/Iraq border. The Saluki type manifests itself from west Africa, through north Africa and what was Mesopotamia, to the Iran/Afghanistan border. Some are used to track game; others to slow game down for the hawk and others to catch desert partridges before they can take off. If anything they are the lurchers of the desert, versatile hunting dogs not just fast runners. They may present a challenge to the impatient but, from their distinguished heritage, have genes worth having. For a while however, their handlers may still have need of a well-fuelled jeep and a good pair of binoculars!

'The Saluki is simply a nomad's lurcher, a provider, a pot filler and it would be wholly wrong to think that such dogs were kept only by oil-rich sheiks. Prior to the overthrow of the Turks during the 1914–1918 war, few sheiks were much richer than the rest of their tribe and ate the same food, following the same lifestyle as did the average tribesman. This is the light in which the traditional owners of the saluki should be regarded...'

Brian Plummer, *The Complete Book of Sight Hounds, Long Dogs and Lurchers*, Robinson, 1991

'The Saluqi, which seems always to have been excepted from the Muslim proscription of dogs, became the favoured hunting companion of the amirs and has remained so to the present day, the amirs having been replaced by the shaikhs, at least in the Arabian peninsula and, in the recent past, in Jordan, Syria and Iraq.'

Michael Rice, *Swifter than the Arrow, The Golden Hunting Hounds of Ancient Egypt*, Tauris, 2006

These Saluki lurchers are bred to function.
(Charwynne Dog Features)

Saluki: ancient breed. (Charwynne Dog Features)

Azawakh, from Mali. (Charwynne Dog Features)

Great extension is the key element.

The Whippet today. (Charwynne Dog Features)

Below: **Racing Whippet.**

THE WHIPPET

Half a century ago, I was working with a group of men from the pit villages of north-east England when the subject of rabbit-dogs came up. One of my colleagues from the south mentioned that his mother showed Whippets and hunted rabbits with them. He was asked how you could put a Whippet in a Kennel Club show when each dog was different. One faction declared that the only true Whippet was the result of a Smooth Fox Terrier crossed with a small Greyhound, back-crossed to a Staffie after five generations. Not one of them would accept that the Whippet was a pure-bred KC-recognised breed with more than ten generations of 'pure' breeding. For them the Whippet had to *function*; its breeding mattered less than its performance.

Against that background, it is interesting to note that in *The Oxford Reference Dictionary* (OUP 1986) a Whippet is defined as: 'a cross-bred dog of Grey-hound type used for racing'. The origin of the word itself is set out as coming from an obsolete word meaning to move briskly. A similar word 'whappet' is defined in the *Dictionary of Archaic Words* of 1850 as 'a prick-eared cur'. Perhaps my northern friends were on to something! There is a quite expensive book on the Whippet which goes to great lengths to try to prove that the Whippet has existed for centuries, using scores of old paintings and sculptures depicting small Greyhound-like dogs as evidence.

Apart from the fact that it is very unwise to talk of pure breeds before the 19th century, it is ludicrous to claim that small sighthounds have to be Whippets. By that measure the Cirneco dell'Etna of Sicily, the South African native hunting dogs, the Pharoah Hound of the Maltese Islands and the small podencos of the Mediterranean littoral would have to come under that name too. Throughout recorded history there have been accounts and depictions of small smooth-haired sighthounds. In England diminutive Greyhounds were long favoured as ladies' companion dogs, quite separately from the delicate Toy breed of Italian Greyhound.

Some will claim that the Whippet *must* have terrier blood to be a genuine Whippet, alleging that the Kennel Club show fraternity hijacked this type, made it into a pedigree breed with a closed gene pool, better named Miniature Greyhound than misappropriating the common name given to the rabbit-dog of the mining community of the north-east. It is too late now to undo this recognition but many find it hard to think of a Whippet as a pure breed. Before the days of kennel clubs in the world, pure breeding from a closed gene pool, whatever the quality of the progeny, would have been laughed off the face of the earth. Distinct breed types were prized of course but mainly because of their prowess not their pedigree.

These remarks are not intended as a criticism of show Whippets, many of whom are devastating hunters, or of their breeders, some of whom know a thing or two about breeding sporting dogs. The Laguna Whippets of Mrs D U McKay have a remarkable field and bench reputation. KC-registered Whippets are regularly coursed, with a determined bunch of knowledgeable devotees behind them. They rather shame the show Greyhound fanciers who rarely test their breed in the field. I simply cannot see the point of admiring a hound designed to catch game using sheer speed if you never wish it to do so. The purpose and the build of such a dog is that of a sprinting machine. A Whippet was once recorded as covering 150 yards in 8.6 seconds; such astounding pace is only achieved if the dog possesses the anatomy which facilitates such remarkable speed.

All sighthounds are 'double-flight' creatures, unlike the horse, a 'single-flight' animal, which for most of its stride, some or all of its hooves are on the ground. The sighthounds race in a series of leaps;

they therefore must have extraordinary extension, fore and aft. This is permitted by the slope of the shoulders on the forehand and the pelvic slope in the hindhand. Long legs and a build like a radiator support this degree of extension. The radiator analogy is deliberate; human beings are good at getting rid of excess heat but not good at storing it. Dogs are just the opposite: very good at storing it, not very good at getting rid of it. Dogs give off excess heat rather as a radiator does, they need adequate surface areas to achieve this. If a Whippet when racing or coursing cannot shed excess heat, they suffer; if they reach a temperature of over 108 degrees they could die.

Much is made in conformation shows of 'heart and lung' room in dogs which sprint as their function. The need for lung room I can understand but heart room? The heart stays the same size even during the greatest exertion. What is never mentioned is liver size. Sprinters run their whole race on sugar mobilised from the liver, liver glycogen. A big liver can store more sugar; sighthounds which run out of liver sugar collapse. It would be worthy research to do post-mortems on the great racing Whippets and Greyhounds and record the weights of their hearts and livers. I would be prepared to bet that these dogs were successful mainly because of their increased heart and liver size. But structure matters too.

After a lack of sheer determination, the biggest fault for me in a sporting Whippet is upright shoulders, so often accompanied by short upper arms. The forward extension determines the forward stride of the dog in the sprint; if you limit that extension you handicap the dog. The shoulder placement is the key to forward movement, well-placed shoulders allow the full forward reach. Any Whippet with a hint of a Hackney-action, that high-stepping prancing front-action of the Toy breed, the Italian Greyhound, should never be bred from. The shoulder blades should almost touch each other at the withers, perhaps one finger's width being usual. I never see ring judges check this feature.

At the back, the falling away at the croup and low-set tail allows full forward reach of the power-house hindquarters, the source of running strength. Any lack of slope in the pelvis and the dog has limited forward reach in the rear legs, a terrible fault. Whippets carry their tails low because of this structural need in a running dog. Spitz breeds don't have to sprint for their keep, but have other needs; they display a high tail set and little slope in the croup. Function has long determined form. But just as the saying 'no hoof, no horse' is a perennial truth in that animal, no foot, no dog, is just as valid. I see far too many Whippets with poor feet, weak, not tight and the dog not 'standing up on them', usually a sign of unfitness through a lack of exercise. I have three books on the Whippet which do not have the words foot or feet in their index; they are rather more important than that.

I am old enough to remember Whippets in British show rings in the 1960s and 1970s when I recall that firstly the quality was high and secondly show judges' critiques did not mention the disappointing findings of recent times. Are we entering an era when show breeders have little concept of what a sporting breed is, an animal designed *to function?* At this rate we could end up with our show Whippets resembling Italian Greyhounds more than their original breed template. If you ally such a concern with the ban on hunting with dogs, then I can only be gloomy about the long-term future of this distinctive little sighthound. The perpetuation of the instinct to hunt at speed, and the anatomy which allows the dog to succeed, matter enormously in such a breed. These are essential building blocks not passing whims.

The Whippet, for its size, may well be the swiftest of all animals. Some years back, in a lecture at the Royal Institution on 'The Dimensions of Animals and Their Muscular Dynamics', Professor A V Hill made a number of salient points. He pointed out that a small animal conducts each of its movements quicker than a large one, with muscles having a higher intrinsic speed and being able proportionately to develop more power. The maximum speeds of the racehorse, Greyhound and Whippet are apparently in the ratio 124:110:110 but their weight relationship is in the ratio 6,000:300:100. The larger animal

Rough haired Lurcher: Whippet x Bedlington. (Charwynne Dog Features)

Whippet eager to run. (Charwynne Dog Features)

Below: **Whippets portrayed in 1900.** (Charwynne Dog Features)

Whippet being judged.

Whippet ready to run. (Charwynne Dog Features)

Blue Streak at the BFSS Country Fair winning the up to 24lb weight class in 1975. This pedigree Whippet, owned by Mrs A A Gaitskell of London, has won once and been finalist twice at the WCRA Champoinships. He is also a show winner, has been to Crufts and is a coursing stake winner with the East of England WCC.
Note the remarkable extension needed to attain this stride.
(Charwynne Dog Features)

Whippet racing at Amsterdam track. Contrast the rear dog with the near dog: extraordinary extension.

Racing Whippet.

however can maintain its pace for longer periods. Professor Hill suggested that up a steep hill, the speed of a racehorse, Greyhound and Whippet could be in reverse order to that on the flat. It is generally held that a Whippet's best performance is over a furlong on the flat, when it can capitalise on its ability to provide the maximum oxygen supply per unit weight of muscle. This is a very powerful animal.

The breed standard of the Whippet refers to this power in its general appearance section: 'Balanced combination of muscular power and strength with elegance and grace of outline. Built for speed and work.' I only wish some of the exhibitors at the shows whose critiques I quoted earlier would heed those key phrases. It is pleasing too to see in this breed standard under colour: 'Any colour or mixture of colours'. This not only gives the breed a rich variety of colours but prevents the absurd colour prejudices which exist in some other breeds. For some pure-breed fanciers the colour is more important than structural soundness. Grattius, writing in the last century BC, gave the view that we should: 'Choose the sighthound pied with black and white; he runs more swift than thought or winged light.' Oppian subsequently wrote that black and white in combination led to 'overheating'. Edward, second Duke of York, stated in 1406 that: 'the best hue is rede fallow, with a black moselle'. It is surely the road to failure if any breeder chooses a sire on the basis of colour.

Colour of coat can however mislead judges, due to a trick of human eyesight. Blacks and blues can appear smaller and more spindly. A dog with a black saddle can appear to have a dippy back. A black patch on the upper arm can give a different impression than a black patch over the withers and down to the brisket. A white underline on an otherwise black dog can make it look shelly. Foreface markings too can create illusions, sometimes shortening the muzzle. Heavy markings on the neck can make it look stuffy when it isn't. Black stockings on a white dog can give a false picture of its gait. Lower leg black markings affect the way the human eye sees leg movement. But if you challenge a judge about such 'trompes d'oeil' the usual response is 'Oh, I can't get fooled like that!' I wonder.

But just as coat colours attract much debate so too does coat texture. There was uproar in the American Whippet scene a few years back when a long-haired Whippet, also known as the Wheeler Whippet, was promoted. Critics of these dogs alleging outcrosses need to keep in mind that sighthounds can feature differing coat textures in the same breed, as the Saluki and Ibizan Hound demonstrate. In Britain we once had a Wold Greyhound which had a long silky coat. Rough-haired Whippets once featured until the show ring and breeder preferences took charge. But far more important than the colour or texture of the coat is its condition. The skin should be loose, pliable and when pinched up should resume its natural state instantly. A tight dry skin is so often a sign of ill-health.

Size is a long-standing debate in the world of the Whippet. A Durham miner once told me that 60 or 70 years ago, his grandfather favoured an 8lb Whippet, 'so's it could fit in y'overcoat pocket'. In the breed standard, a male Whippet can be from 18½ to 20 inches high. Such a dog might weigh around 21lb. The Whippet Club Racing Association height limit is 21 inches; coursing Whippets must go under the measure at 20 inches. Bigger dogs seem to be favoured in North America. No doubt in time we will see an American Whippet achieve recognition as a 22 inch specimen, rather as American Bulldogs are bigger than ours or the French variety. I have no problem with sportsmen seeking a hound to suit their terrain but this would be a Miniature Greyhound not a Whippet.

Some years ago, writing in the dog press, Ted Walsh, who knew a bit about Whippets, stated: 'A coursing dog should be judged on movement first, balance second, and make and shape last; if the first two are right, there shouldn't be much wrong with the third.' He also expressed his dismay at some of the dogs presented in the show ring, stating that they 'couldn't catch a cat in a kitchen'. There is rather more to a winning Whippet than a roach back, hyper-angulation in the hindlegs, a straight front and open feet, yet dogs with such features seem to be able to qualify for Crufts; I share Ted Walsh's dismay. Writing in the Whippet Club's Jubilee Show catalogue

Ch Lily of Laguna.

Ch Laguna Ligonier.

Whippets, 1898.

Nigel Wallbank's Lady of Rabbitrunner and Pennymeadow Penny after a 2006 winter session.
(From Nigel Wallbank and Jeff Hutchings' excellent publication *The Working Whippet Yearbook 2007*)

The Whippet features a wide variety of coat colours.
(Charwynne Dog Features)

in 1950, W Lewis Renwick declared that: 'Another important thing to remember is what the breed is bred for. Firstly, he is not a lady's pet dog, despite the fact that no more affectionate breed exists and no dog is happier than when living in the comfort of his master's home. He is first and last a Sporting Dog, his conformation being for great speed over short distances... anybody who has an eye for beauty of form and muscular development must admit there are few dogs so artistic to look upon.' These are important words for any Whippet breeder to have in his mind. The Whippet is a canine athlete or it is nothing. As the sporting dog comes under the threat from 'town-thinking' people over its use in the field, we should keep in mind that this breed wasn't evolved for the squires in their shires, but developed by hard-working miners in humble pit villages. No smart-ass Irish playright could accuse them of being 'the unspeakable in full pursuit of the uneatable'. I pray that Whippets will be catching rabbits, which are very eatable, for many centuries to come and contributing their blood to create improved lurchers too.

The Whippet of 1904: stronger-boned, squarer-built.
(Charwynne Dog Features)

English Deerhound, depicted over the entrance to Saltram House, Plymouth. (Charwynne Dog Features)

Highland Greyhound or Wolf Dog.

Deer lurchers at work. Detail from *Diana and her Nymphs Hunting Deer*, Circle of Paul de Vos, oil on canvas. (Charwynne Dog Features)

THE LOSS OF THE ENGLISH DEERHOUND

In the Middle Ages, thousands and thousands of 'strong Greyhounds', both rough-coated and smooth, were used to course deer in Scotland, Ireland and England. The Scottish version developed into the Deerhound breed of today; the Irish dog contributed to the Irish Wolfhound of today. The English dog became in type what today we would call a lurcher. Hunting deer with scenthounds became the preferred style and the English deerhound found a home with the lower order of hunter, the peasant class. But there is plenty of evidence of this hound, in statues, paintings and prints. Of interest to lurchermen is the account of Irish Greyhounds recorded by Fitzinger in his *Der Hund* of 1876: 'The Irish Greyhound, next to the Indian and Russian Greyhound, is the largest specimen of the Greyhound type, combining the speed of the Greyhound with the size of the Mastiff. The second type is the Irish coursing dog, a cross between the Irish Greyhound and the Mastiff or bandogge. He is shorter in the neck with a coarser skull, broader chest, and heavily flewed lips.' He went on to describe a third variety: a cross between the Irish Greyhound and the shepherd dog, shaggy-coated and lower on the leg. He could have been writing about coarsely bred hunting sighthounds in England of past centuries too. The surviving British breed of Deerhound, the Scottish hound, retains many of the characteristics of the old native hunting sighthounds and gives us an idea of their capabilities.

In his *The Scottish Deerhound* of 1892, the authoritative Weston Bell wrote: 'for the work this dog had to do, if we take his general appearance at over 30 inches, he would be almost too heavy and clumsy, but no doubt could hold a stag better than a lighter dog, though he would not have the same staying power that a lighter dog would have. For bitches the height should be from 26 to 27 inches at the shoulder'. But the Kennel Club's standard for the Deerhound lays down a minimum desirable height at withers of 30 inches for dogs and 28 inches for bitches. In 1880 Thomas Morse's famous bitch Spey was precisely measured at eleven years old, with these dimensions: Weight 73 lbs, height at shoulder 26 inches, girth of neck 15 inches, girth around shoulders 30 inches, girth of loins 21 inches, girth of thigh 16 inches, height at elbow 14 inches, height at loins 26 inches. It is worth noting that the height at shoulder and loin is the same. All these dimensions have value for lurchermen, especially those favouring the staghound lurcher. It is also worth remembering that the early show Deerhounds were often those too big to make a successful hunting dog; size is of no value by itself for dogs expected to function.

In his *The Illustrated Book of the Dog*, of 1879, Vero Shaw quotes the distinguished Scottish sportsman, Sir John McNiel, as saying, of his Deerhounds, in 1868: 'The largest and finest dog I ever bred or ever saw was my Oscar. His speed was such that in a straight run he was never beaten by any dog, rough or smooth; and in his best condition he weighed ninety-four pounds...' He also quotes another renowned Scottish nobleman-hunter as saying, of his celebrated strain of Deerhounds: 'I have never had in my possession a dog above 31 inches...' stating that he had seen one 34 inches in height which was an 'utterly useless animal'! In *The Pursuit of Wild Animals for Sport*, of 1856, J H Walsh writes of a deer hunt with: 'Suffice it to remark, that after the dogs were slipped, a long and severe course ensued, in which various casualties took place, incidental to such rough and rocky ground. At the termination of the course, when the party arrived at the spot where the deer lay, the hound was perfectly exhausted, and had lain down, shaking from head to foot like a broken-down horse...' He recorded that this particular hound, before he was a year old, had killed a full-grown hind single-handed. The hounds which coursed deer, whether in Scotland or England, were remarkable dogs.

Lurcher fanciers would enjoy the words of 'Stonehenge' in *The Dogs of the British Islands*, of 1878: '...with the disappearance of the rough greyhound has been the rarity of the deerhound in modern days, the former being displaced by the smooth breed, and the latter by various crosses, e.g., that between the foxhound and greyhound advocated by Mr Scrope; the mastiff and greyhound cross of the Earl of Stamford, and all sorts of crosses between the colley and greyhound, rough as well as smooth, as mentioned above. In the present day pure deer-hounds kept for the retrieving of deer are compara-tively rare, and I believe even those in Her Majesty's kennel are not used for that purpose. Hence it is idle to attempt to describe this dog solely from the deer-stalker's point of view, and he must be estimated rather from an artistic standpoint, in which capacity he rivals, and perhaps surpasses, all his brethren, having the elegant frame of the greyhound united with the rough shaggy coat, which takes off the hard-ness of outline complained of by the lovers of the picturesque as attaching to the English "longtail".'

It is easy to overlook the value as well as the prowess of hounds which could hunt red deer suc-cessfully before the wide use of long range firearms. The red deer is the largest of Britain's wild mammals, a mature stag measuring four feet at the shoulder and weighing around 300lb. In a harsh winter the skill of such a dog could mean the difference between star-vation and survival for the primitive hunters. Once this value diminished, however, these huge shaggy fast-running hounds fell on hard times, surviving only in some areas through the patronage of the nobility. In *Medieval Hunting* (Sutton, 2003) Richard Almond writes: 'This is undoubtedly due to the change in role of greyhounds by the eighteenth century, from that of hunting deer, hare, wolf, boar and fox to that of coursing hares in organised matches.' He wrote too that 'Deer were obvious targets for peasant poachers... Recent research into the thirteenth and fourteenth century records of the Forest courts reveals that peasants poached deer not only for immediate consumption but for future pleas-ures too, such as a family wedding feast or Christmas dinner...' Deer poaching would have entailed the use of fast, strong Greyhound-type dogs – English Deerhounds or lurchers!

The ancient employment of Deerhounds in Scotland involved a brace coursing their quarry and killing it unaided. Single-handed killing was no mean feat; the famous working Deerhound Bran, in 1844, killed two unwounded stags in about 45 minutes. Such a hunting accomplishment demands not just resolution, commitment, speed, strength and stamina but physically sound, superbly constructed dogs, whose limbs and, especially their feet, can cope with boulder-strewn terrain at speed, whose joints can withstand fierce and repeated jarring and whose physique blends great power with lightness of build. The first point I look for in a moving Deerhound, even in a show ring, is a discernible springiness of step and 'daisy-clipping' action in the feet; this indi-cates for me a basic soundness. A high leg-lift is tiring for a hunting dog; it is rooted in incorrect hind construction. It is also ugly movement, detracting from the flowing gait all sporting dogs need. At a championship dog show a couple of years ago, the Deerhound judge's critique read: 'Far too many dogs and bitches are too fine and lacking in substance to enable them to do the job they were bred for. Many of the youngsters had poor fronts, while many older hounds lacked drive from the rear...' Another at a different show commented on the unsound move-ment and a lack of fore-chest. This is depressing reading in an ancient hunting breed.

In his *Encyclopaedia of Rural Sports* of 1870, Delabere Blaine records, on deer hunting, that 'In feudal times... from five hundred to a thousand were sometimes slain at one general hunting match... As late as the third century, the Britons who had remained unconquered, and lived beyond Adrian's wall, were principally supported by venison...' The call for hounds must have been remarkable. The worth of the best hounds would have been consid-erable, but they were valued for what they could do, not their statuesque appearance, any air of nobility or aloof grandeur, as flowery breed descriptions of today can hint. Sighthounds specialising in deer-hunting were once very much part of England's sporting canine scene. Lord Ribblesdale in his book

Deerhounds by function (lurchers) *Death of the Roebuck* **by Paul de Vos.**

English Deerhound of 1800.

This portrayal of a 17th century deer-hunt depicts the coarsely bred deer lurchers used at that time all over Europe.
(Charwynne Dog Features)

The Queen's Hounds, wrote that 'a breed of deer-hounds were long preserved at Godmersham and Eastwell in Kent, the strain of which went back to Elizabethan days. A good one always pinned the deer by the ear, a criterion of the purity of the strain. They were cream or fawn-coloured, with dusky muzzles, greyhound speed and half-greyhound, half-mastiff like heads.' Some bull lurchers of today would answer that description. Deer hounds don't have to be rough-coated and Scottish!

In his book *The Rifle and Hound in Ceylon* (Longman's, 1890) Sir Samuel Baker wrote of using a cross between the Foxhound and the Bloodhound for elk-hunting. The elk is the largest living deer, about the size of a larger horse in the hunting field. (Baker used Deerhound crosses on sambur deer.) He wrote that ' The only important drawback to elk-hunting is the constant loss of the dogs. The best is always sure to go. What with deaths by boars, leopards, elk and stray hounds, the pack is with difficulty maintained.' In pre-war India, sportsmen noted that the local sighthounds, like the Banjara, the Mudhol, the Vaghari and the Rampur, always went for the deer's hindquarters, whereas the imported Deerhounds seized by the throat. One day soon we will have lost all our dogs with hunting instincts like this, and who can say they will never be needed again?

Who would dare to steal sheep if we still had our shepherds' mastiffs, living constantly with the flocks? Equivalent pastoral dogs, like the Anatolian Shepherd Dog, are being introduced into African flocks to protect against marauding members of the cat family, with measurable effect. Sporting dogs don't have to be conserved solely by bodies like the Kennel Club, with their major outing being to Crufts, now very appropriately to be sponsored by a sofa manufacturer. But it is individual native enthusiasts who should be stepping forward. The admirably intentioned Native Dog Breeds Trust has now been wound up through lack of support. No doubt a foreign 'deerhound', with an invented provenance and little merit, is about to be imported. The English Deerhound lives on in the lurcher ranks but shame on us for losing such a distinctive and valuable type of hound.

English Deerhound with catch-dog of 1820. Charles Towne's depiction of a fawn, black-masked, crop-eared catch-dog of 1820. (Charwynne Dog Features)

CHAPTER 4

FIELDING THE LURCHER

The Show Ring Dog
Hunting the Rabbit
Bobbery Packs
Shouldering Responsibility
Learning about Loins

Who wants to win with an unworthy dog?
(Charwynne Dog Features)

Well stacked dog. (Charwynne Dog Features)

M Salkeld's Blue, on left, T Dunn's Gyp, on right.

THE SHOW RING DOG

Why show lurchers? Does it identify future breeding stock or merely parade dogs bred to look good? What ever the purpose, lurcher shows do provide a great day out for the country sports enthusiast. There are a number of aspects of lurcher shows which concern me. Firstly, some are not well organised and this is discourteous to lurcher owners who have travelled a long way to be there and paid good money to enter the site and the ring. Secondly, the standard of judging is too varied, ranging from the competent to the inadequate; this insults the patronage of worthy fanciers and degrades the sport. Thirdly, far too many entries are ill-prepared both in show-training and condition. What really is the point of entering such a show if the dog can't be handled or is not in show condition?

In his book *All About the Bull Terrier*, the much-missed Tom Horner recorded: 'A wise breeder puts on show only his best stock and presents them in the peak of condition, physically fit, clean and trained to show off their points.' Moaning about the quality of the judging is misplaced if your exhibit has not been prepared for the show. This is a matter of personal standards and reflects badly when detected on any lurcher exhibitor. Witnessing a lurcher being awarded a prize when unbrushed, unschooled and under-exercised does nothing for one's confidence in future lurcher breeding.

In his informative *The Practical Guide to Showing Dogs* of 1956, Captain Portman-Graham wrote: 'The fact that a dog is structurally sound is not in itself sufficient to ensure that it will always win at shows. It is of paramount importance that it must be... at the highest standard of condition. Perhaps one of the biggest advantages which dog showing confers on the dog as an animal is the care which must be bestowed upon it.' If unfit dogs with poor muscular condition can win at dog shows, then the whole argument that such shows improve dogs is totally destroyed. Dogs which are inadequately exercised and merely wheeled out for the next show can be so easily identified by any competent judge and quickly thrown out of the ring that such an insidious practice, both for dogs and the dog game, can be ended. Are our current crop of judges up to this?

The esteemed Portman-Graham went on to write: '...exercise is a vital consideration in maintaining any breed of show dog in bloom, health and vigour... When one watches the beautiful muscles of a race-horse one sees a similarity between a dog's muscles which have been developed correctly and naturally, and ripple in movement.' Yet there is evidence of lack of muscular tone and development at many lurcher shows today.

But what is actually meant by the expression 'show condition'? The Kennel Club's Glossary of Terms defines condition as: 'Health as shown by the body, coat, general appearance and deportment. Denoting overall fitness.' The last phrase is the key one. Frank Jackson, in his most useful *Dictionary of Canine Terms*, defines condition as: 'Quality of health evident in coat, muscle, vitality and general demeanour.' Harold Spira, in his *Canine Terminology*, describes it as: 'An animal's state of fitness or health as reflected by external appearance and behaviour. For example, muscular development...' The Breed Standards and Stud Book Sub-Committee at the KC inform me that show condition indicated an expectation of 'a dog in good health as indicated by good coat condition, good muscle tone, a bright eye and up on the feet', adding that any competent judge would know this. One thing is inescapable in the interpretation of these definitions, condition means fitness as demonstrated in the dog's muscular state. If entries at KC shows have to be fit, then surely our lurchers have to be super-fit. Shouldn't they be anyway?

One final point concerns what might be termed 'fashion of the day', in which some transient whim

Lurcher day out.

A mixed bag in a lurcher class. (Charwynne Dog Features)

Mr A Jeffrey of Carlisle with his Champion lurcher, centre, with reserve prizewinner Mr B Addison of Chester-le-Street.

becomes the big deal for a while. Upright shoulders can make a dog look statuesque 'on the flags'; over-angulation can make a hound look as though it's 'covering a lot of ground'; stringing the exhibit up on a choke-chain tight to its throat can make a dog look nobler, to some. None of these passing whims has anything to do with sane honest worthy presentation and are not good for the dog. In the superficial purpose of winning at all costs, some exhibitors forget they are handling functional creatures and pursue foolish aims which actually harm the dog.

The respected greyhound expert H Edwards Clarke once wrote: '...perhaps the greatest fetish of the show ring is that the greyhound must be shown with lean shoulders. As galloping naturally develops muscle in the shoulders, the simple solution was that the greyhound destined for the bench must not be allowed to gallop.' Show fanciers were once advised to gallop their hounds uphill but walk them down, so that ribs, loin and hindquarters were developed but not the shoulders. It is this kind of misguided thinking which leads in different ways in different breeds to faulty development and the unwise selection of breeding stock. Once function is lost so too is type, soundness and the relationship between terrain, quarry and that function. Lurchermen know better; the pot has to be filled.

'It would be in vain to look for the Lurcher in the streets or parks of London, in any of our considerable towns, or any of our dog shows... the Lurcher is, in fact, par excellence the poacher's dog, and those who desire to see him must look for him in the rural districts...'

Hugh Dalziel, *British Dogs*, Upcott Gill, 1888

'Shows certainly have their uses... Longdog hybrids win most of the events, however, and justly so, for being a mixture of sight hounds they possess none of the less appealing elements imparted by a cross which involves non-sight hounds. The truth is that some long-dogs are extraordinarily handsome.'

Brian Plummer, *The Complete Book of Sight Hounds, Long Dogs and Lurchers*, Robinson, 1991

Lurcher judging. (Charwynne Dog Features)

Waiting for the judge. (Charwynne Dog Features)

Judge at work. (Charwynne Dog Features)

RETRIEVING LURCHER

'As this dog possesses the advantage of a fine scent, it is often employed in killing hares and rabbits in the night time. When taken to the warren, it steals out with the utmost precaution, watches and scents the rabbits while they are feeding, and darts upon them without barking or making the least noise.'

Thomas Bewick on the lurcher, in his *A General History of Quadrupeds* of 1790

Airedale–Teckel cross. An attempt to breed a rabbit dog, Germany 1922.

Landscape with Rabbit Hunters **Sebastian Vrancx, 1753–1647.** (Charwynne Dog Features)

HUNTING THE RABBIT

The charming book *Watership Down*, along with the enchanting film *Bambi*, did much to provide the urban-dwelling public with a wholly misleading view of man and nature. In a crowded island, deer need controlling, in their own interests. Bunnies are not cute; they are a nuisance, an expensive nuisance. The wild rabbit is one of the greatest pests in Britain and yet it has not been one to earn its own specialised breed of dog for its control or extermination. We have Fox Terriers, Otter Hounds and now Minkhounds, Wolfhounds and Deerhounds but not, by name, Rabbit Hounds. I realise that the Bedlington Terrier, the Whippet and the Beagle can hunt rabbits very effectively, quite apart from working terriers and lurchers, but it is surprising that the rabbit itself has not drawn a specialist in title. The lurcher is a supreme rabbit-hunter but has a capability beyond just that.

Under The Hunting Act of 2004, rabbit hunting is exempt so long as it takes place on your own land or you have the landowner's permission to do so. Find me a landowner who welcomes rabbits on his land and he will be immediately shown up as someone with little or no knowledge of the extensive damage they do. Years ago, one prominent estate owner was reported as having committed suicide, with his dying words recorded as 'The rabbits have killed me!' Half a century ago, one expert estimated that there were 100 million rabbits in Britain. With each doe capable of producing 36 fast-maturing offspring a year, rabbits are responsible for a 17% loss in agricultural yield, averaging in some places £40 per acre per year. Rabbit-proof fencing and chemical extermination is costly and never a one-off measure. Send for the rabbit hunters!

At the start of the last century, one enthusiast here imported a Portuguese Warren Hound, one of the Podengo breeds of all-round sporting dogs from Southern Europe. It didn't gain supporters; if it had been imported under its proper title: Portuguese Rabbit Dog, it might have done better, there's a lot to a name. In the last few years, Betty Judge has brought in a number of the small variety of the Portuguese Podengo. They look a little like Cairn Terriers, but are commendably nondescript, with no fancy coats, special heads or breed features for the exaggerators to get excited about. They are alert, robust, keen-eyed and determined little sporting dogs, worth a glance from breeders of small lurchers.

When I was in Portugal fairly regularly some thirty years ago, I was impressed by both the medium-sized and the small-sized Portuguese Rabbit Dogs; they were brilliant at hunting rabbits in trying conditions, where there are dry stone walls and terraces, which provide enormous scope for agile rabbits. Similar podengos can be found all along the Mediterranean littoral. I found a remarkably similar hunting dog in Malta and Gozo half a century ago, where a pack of local hounds, strengthened by a red Whippet and a tan Manchester Terrier, left behind by departing servicemen, provided great hunting. Their agility was hugely impressive.

Years later, I was amused to note that a British enthusiast had imported some Maltese Rabbit Dogs and persuaded our Kennel Club to name them 'Pharoah Hounds', with a foolishly conceived provenance linking them directly with ancient Egyptian hunting dogs. No one makes such a claim for the other breeds of this exact type, found in Crete, Sicily, the Spanish Islands (as the Ibizan Hound demonstrates), Spain or Portugal. The little bobbery pack of Gozoan Hounds which impressed me when hunting rabbit, in terrain demanding great agility and hunting skill, didn't deserve such shabby treatment; I don't know of a single one, of those imported here and subsequently bred from, being used here on rabbit.

A blend of Whippet, Manchester Terrier and Portuguese Podengo would produce a very effective rabbit lurcher here. No doubt there are small lurchers of such a type being used already; there are examples of this type at most big lurcher shows. With the historic hare-hounds affected by the Hunting with Dogs legislation, a specialist hound, dedicated to vermin control, might have a brighter future. Rabbit-hunting has long been sniffed at by the well-heeled sportsmen, but times have changed, country sports have to be reshaped, the day of the rabbit-hunter may have arrived.

In the United States, the American Rabbit Hound Association registers rabbit hounds bred to meet its standards. Founded in 1986, with 140 clubs in over 28 states, the ARHA promotes hunting competitions and offers a programme of organised rabbit hound hunts. There are six types of hunt competitions: gundog brace, gundog pack, big pack, little pack, progressive pack and Basset. The objective of these field events is to identify those hounds with the best ability to search (i.e. locate the rabbit), flush and drive the rabbit back to the hunter. At the end of each hunt competition, there is a conformation show to try to identify the best constructed hounds. A comparable parent body here might concentrate the minds of rabbit-hunters.

Britons holidaying in the Canaries may under-rate the sporting potential there; but the Podencos Canarios, or hunting dogs, find plenty of sport on rabbit there, even in Lanzarote. This type of sporting dog is found too in Majorca, as well as Ibiza. The rabbits there don't live underground but in crevices, piles of rocks or in crumbling stone walls. As both the late Brian Plummer and Ted Walsh frequently pointed out, catching rabbits above ground is never easy. They may be classed as vermin and sneered at by the more privileged hunter but they can make a good hare-dog look stupid. The Sicilians pride their rabbit-dog, the Cirneco dell'Etna, on its scenting skill just as much as its speed and agility. Dry stone walls and rocky hillsides really test a dog's hunting ability. Volcanic lava really tests a dog's feet. The rabbit is worthy prey; I actually prefer rabbit pie to jugged hare. The day of the rabbit-dog may have arrived!

Hunters have long controlled rabbits using 'bobbery' packs of terriers, Beagles and Whippets, as well as small lurchers. In his *Beagle and Terrier* of 1946, Roger Free recommended a small pack of Beagles for rabbit control. He wrote that: 'they have the advantage of being absolutely tireless in their pursuit of the elusive rabbit and add to the day a touch of colour and music which would otherwise be missing.' Sir Jocelyn Lucas ran Beagles with his terrier pack to encourage them to give tongue. Lucas related, in 1909, how a sportsman approached him with an offer to sell him tiny miniature Dachshunds, which he claimed were small enough to go below ground and draw a rabbit. Lucas stated that these Dachshunds were small enough to negotiate a 4 inch wicker pipe!

A century ago, Hutchinson, the great gundog expert, recorded one sportsman using 'the smallest Beagles that can be obtained' on rabbits, ones that were trained to ignore hares – as they would have to be today. But he strongly advised against the use of spaniels to hunt them, arguing: 'As for rabbits, I beg we may have no further acquaintance if you ever, even in imagination, shoot them to your young dog... He will degenerate into a low potterer – a regular hedge-hunter. In turnips he will always be thinking more of rabbits than birds.' But I have known of a brace of Sussex Spaniels being used by a rough shooter on rabbit and feathered game, without any loss of control or specialisation. The dogs seemed to know how to hunt each quarry differently.

In his *The Dog in Sport* of 1938, James Wentworth Day wrote of an old Sussex squire who 'bred and kept the Sussex Spaniel. Now that is a rather heavy sort of spaniel, with a nice, shining coat, bred to hunt rabbits out of those vast beds of gorse which cover the Sussex Downs with a golden sheet...' He is said to have trained them to hunt the South Down rabbit, just as a neighbouring squire did with a pack of Beagles. The spaniels in the Sussex pack wore bells on their collars so the squire could hear where they were hunting, normally out of sight. Wentworth Day also greatly admired the rabbit-hunting Sealyham pack of Sir Jocelyn Lucas. He wrote that 'They brought hard-bitten, hard-riding Essex farmers out of their stackyards and stockyards to gaze in admiration, to voice naive praise'.

Delabere Blaine, in his *Rural Sports* of 1870, also

Gozo, 1956: Local 'Rabbit Dogs'. (Charwynne Dog Features)

LEFT: **Do the public really prefer to have rabbits gassed or snared?**

Warreners at Barnham, Sufolk, in 1921 with dogs. (Norfolk Museums Service NRLM, Gressenhall)

admired the sight of spaniels hunting the rabbit. He wrote of 'The spaniels questing for rabbits within the close tanglings of an extensive wood; their merry cry bespeaks them on the scent; the sporting attendants spread here and there, all eye, and all ear, to see the quick darting of the rabbit across the path... the nimble spaniel is seen racing over the same tract in his wake.' Such a country activity used to prevent many a feckless youth from suffering the boredom of the teenaged years – the sheer enthusiasm of the dogs alone stirring the blood. In his book, also entitled *Rural Sports*, of 1801, William Daniel writes of one wildlife expert who calculated that one rabbit could, over a four-year period, initiate the breeding of 478,062 offspring. Plenty of work experience there for bored teenagers!

The late Brian Plummer found terriers best for catching 'sitting' rabbits, superior to sight or scent hounds. He was against going rabbiting with lurchers and terriers together, claiming that fights soon ensued when the faster lurcher stole the terriers' chosen target. But, he, a highly experienced hunter, cautioned against under-rating the rabbit as quarry. He wrote: 'Make no mistake about it... the sighthound has a tough time catching rabbits during daylight hours. Rabbits run quickly, about 25 mph as their top speed... but they reach their top speed in seconds. Run in daylight hours, they dodge and duck well enough to put a hare to shame and seldom feed far from home. Rabbits are never easy catches.'

In Australia they have an even bigger problem with rabbit damage than we do here. Yet, despite developing their own heeler and terrier, they too have never produced a specialist rabbit hound by name. This may be because the breeds taken there from Britain were deemed adequate for the task. In his informative book *Australian Barkers and Biters* of 1914, Robert Kaleski paid tribute to the Beagle, writing: 'Of late years another job has arisen for the Beagle in Australia, and he, like all good Australians, has risen to the job. This job is a very important one. Every grazier knows that after his country has been absolutely swept bare of the grey curse there is invariably one here and one there overlooked in some inaccessible places which pop up and start breeding

again. Ordinary dogs do not bother with odd ones like these in bad places; but the Beagle, with whom chasing rabbits is an age-old instinct, goes after these 'last rabbits' with joy and never leaves them alone until run down and secured.'

It is this sheer persistence, massive enthusiasm and scenting prowess which makes the Beagle such a superlative hunter – and a handful sometimes for a novice Beagle owner not versed in their avid trailing instincts whenever strong scent is encountered! These instincts are being perpetuated by the working section of the Beagle Club and I applaud their efforts in these difficult days for sporting breeds. Perhaps legislation is around the corner for pastoral breeds too; after all sheep farmers do exploit working sheepdogs! Single-issue lobbyists know no bounds nowadays. But lining up urban-dwellers against countrymen is destructively divisive. I always oppose disparaging remarks about 'townees' by countrymen. There is nothing wrong with people who live in towns, but a lot wrong with what Van der Post labelled 'town-mindedness'. We need those who understand dogs that work, whether in the sporting field or the pastures, to step forward and educate those who don't.

I strongly supported the Wild Mammals (Protection) (Amendment) Bill, a much better way of combating human misdeed. The Hunting with Dogs Act is more an act of vengeance than animal welfare. It needs a rethink. I agree with the words of Charles Pye-Smith in his masterly eye-opening recently published *Rural Rites*: 'In its place we need legislation which recognises that the welfare of animals, the well-being of people, and the richness and integrity of the natural world are inextricably linked.' I am saddened by the increasing number of both foxes and hares being found maimed but still alive, following the use of the gun to control their numbers. Before the League of Leporine Rights insists on the country being taken over by rapid-breeding rabbits, those with knowledge of hunting and with humane instincts towards wildlife have much to do. Dogs kill rats faster than poison; dogs catch rabbits cleanly. Lurchers will always be not just the best option but the most humane.

'The lurcher is a dog seldom found in the possession of the honourable sportsman... In a rabbit-warren this dog is peculiarly destructive. His scent enables him to follow them silently and swiftly. He darts unexpectedly upon them, and, being trained to bring his prey to his master, one of these dogs will often in one night supply the poacher with rabbits and other game worth more money than he could earn by two days' hard labour.'

William Youatt, *The Dog*, Longman, Brown, Green and Longmans, 1854

'The dedicated poacher reared lurchers (crossbred dogs trained to hunt silently) and greyhounds which were released into the warren to pick off and retrieve conies one by one... Rabbit poaching was so lucrative that, inevitably, highly organised gangs were formed, operating on a large scale in the bigger warrens of the Breakland.'

Richard Almond, *Medieval Hunting*, Sutton Publishing, 2003

'Most working whippets are jealous dogs and two or three together will go down a hedge, getting faster and faster until they get to the end, when they have to come back more slowly to try for the rabbits they have overrun. This is very difficult to stop and the answer is let one loose at a time until it marks. The others will have spotted the 'mark' before you have done and will go straight to it as soon as they are loosed.'

EG Walsh and Mary Lowe, *The English Whippet*, The Boydell Press, 1984

Coursing greyhound c1900 in better condition than today's Sighthounds.
COURSING DEATHS
In a normal coursing season, of the 2000 hares coursed, only 300 were killed; during such a season, on non-coursing estates, a total of around 394,000 hares would have been shot annually.

Historic country scene: A severe course ensued up and down the hills, the fox-hound coming in for his turn occasionally.

Black-mouthed curs.

The Pack.

BOBBERY PACKS

Lurchers have long formed a key element in the make-up of ad hoc or 'bobbery' packs of sporting dogs. Whatever the outcome of the Hunting with Dogs legislation, there will always be a need for vermin control. This could lead to the licensing of small operators, using dogs and guns, to reduce fox and rabbit numbers in specified areas. However unsatisfactory on the whole for the use of dogs in the hunting field, it could see an increase in the number of 'bobbery packs', usually collections of small hounds and terriers, to drive vermin to the waiting guns.

Ever since reading Roger Free's *Beagle and Terrier* as a fourteen year old, hunting with a small pack of assorted dogs has appealed to me. He wrote in times when individual freedom had greater respect but a future need for vermin control could see his style of operating in the field on the way back and to a greater degree. The remarkable Sir Jocelyn Lucas used to hunt with his renowned Ilmer pack of Sealyhams. Lucas wrote that he didn't want a dog that becomes tired after walking a mile and lamented the 'most appalling-looking terriers described as 'working type'.' There is no need for a bobbery pack to feature unsound dogs or ugly brutes.

Roger Free kept and hunted a small mixed pack of 14 inch Beagles and Terriers for hunting rabbits for the gun. 'Dalesman' described Free's pack as one 'which any huntsman might be proud, because they have all those attributes which go towards excellence. Some of these are bred in the hounds – courage, stamina, nose and tongue – but the rest must be taught and instilled with patience and knowledge of hounds and their work.' But what a challenging self-set task for any ambitious sportsman. Free, not surprisingly, considered that more pleasure was to be derived from hunting your own hounds than from being a follower of a pack hunted by another.

Free argued that whereas gundogs are taught by man, scenthounds frequently learn to hunt without the assistance of man and are therefore more self-reliant. He wasn't decrying the merits of gundogs but stressing the need for a different approach to the training of hounds. He advocated choosing a dog which was not afraid to look you in the eye. He preferred to guide a dog rather than 'break' it. He looked for boldness, perseverance, eagerness and biddability. He emphasised the latter and was aware of the menace of self-hunting hounds, oblivious to all recall. He trained his terriers the same way as his hounds and used Lakeland or Fell Terriers, but was always worried about their colour concealing their whereabouts from the guns.

He concentrated on hunting the hounds and did not himself carry a gun. He normally used four or five couples of Beagles with two or three terriers, finding the latter better in really difficult cover. This meant handling a dozen dogs singlehanded, a testing task. Some sportsmen find controlling one gundog quite beyond them! Generally speaking, terriers and scenthounds demand far more skill in their training than gundogs, partly because of their different instincts and partly because they are often expected to operate in the field *as a pack*. Gundogs have been bred for centuries to respond to human direction in the field; terriers and scenthounds have striven for several centuries to defy all human instructions!

In his informative *Secrets of Dog Training* Brian Plummer writes, with deliberate understatement, 'Terriers despite their small size, are sometimes far from easy to control. In addition to the fact that most terriers still retain a strong inclination to hunt any type of animal or bird whose scent crosses their paths, the majority are particularly eager to take offence from another dog.' It is interesting to note that most experienced and well-regarded terriermen dislike dogs that are too hard; many outspoken but less experienced working terrier fanciers will often boast of the sheer aggression in their dogs. This to me is a sure sign of tongue preceding brain.

Small-time hunting, with a small pack of hunting dogs, does of course take place all over the world. In less crowded countries all sorts of quarry are hunted. In the United States, coon-hunting is conducted from the beaches of Florida to the drains of Michigan. Sometimes pure-bred hounds like the Black and Tan, the Redbone, the Treeing Walker, the Plott and the Bluetick are used. Less well known breeds like the Catahoula Leopard Dog and the Black Mouth Cur are also utilised. American coonhound breeders have found that the open-trailing tendency is dominant over still-trailing, a lack of quality voice is dominant over the beautiful classic hound 'music' and the tendency towards poor scenting ability is dominant over keenness of scent. Breeding plans therefore need great care.

These hunters have tried bird-dogs for their hunts but not surprisingly found that they hunted with their heads up and an inclination to quarter rather than trail. Springer Spaniels have been proven to be good trailers and to cross successfully with hounds. Contrary to expectations, these crosses did not produce good coonhounds: Irish Setter X Blood-hound, Pointer X Bloodhound, English Setter X Foxhound and Pointer X Foxhound. Crosses between farm Collies and hounds produced sound coon-hunting dogs, displaying pace, eagerness, stamina and voice, which although lacking the mellowness of pure hound music carried well over long distances. This is valued in this form of hunting.

A breed no longer used here in Britain for sport-ing purposes but found useful overseas is the Airedale. Perhaps it was a mistake to call this breed a terrier; in France it would have been called a griffon, and expected to hunt the bigger game. The Airedale is appreciated much more in the United States as a working dog than here, the country which produced it. Fifteen years ago the first annual Hunting/Working Workshop of the Airedale Club of America was held. This workshop planned events to prove that the Airedale could still be a versatile hunting dog. In three days, on the Killdeer Plains Wildlife Area near Marion, Ohio, the Airedales were tested in upland bird hunting, trailing and tracking fur and then retrieving.

Then the North American Working Airedale Terrier Association was formed with these goals: to improve the physical soundness and temperament of the breed, to participate in Schutzhund or protection dog training, to promote tracking events and other working tests. I know of no such tests in Britain. For anyone forming a bobbery pack for mink, the Airedale would be a good choice. I wonder though just how dormant the hunting instinct is after a century of neglect. The breed was developed to combat the prevalence of pine-martens (now being reintroduced), polecats and otter in the Aire Valley around 1850.

Breed historians still claim a part-ancestry with the Otterhound, the type stabilised in the packs. I am not convinced. There was a northern hound breed, identified in the middle of the 19th century as the Lancashire Otterhound, black and tan and *wire*-coated. This hound had a distinguished record against water-based vermin and possessed a distinct breed type. The early Airedales had larger ears and a denser, closer waterproof coat. It would be a source of great pleasure to all those who mourn the loss of our Airedale as a *sporting* terrier to see this admirable native breed employed in the hunting field once again.

In his *The Dog in Sport* of 1938, J Wentworth Day wrote: 'Nobody shoots rabbits on sunny Sussex downlands with such packs of slow and musical beagles in these hurried days. We hurry so much we miss the half of life, the charm of quiet things, the simplicity of the easily attainable.' Roger Free knew of the charm of quiet things and found them easily attainable. If packs of hounds ever have to be dispersed, a hunting future in bobbery packs would be one way of employing the best bred dogs in Britain – and perpetuating their ingrained skills. Perhaps those filling their wallets but missing the half of life in the City should now be seeking a country property and a dozen sporting dogs to restore their sanity. In so doing they would be going down a well-worn and rewarding trail. Here's to the future of bobbery packs!

'The sort I have used is, I fancy, a cross of the regular Scotch terrier and the old English beagle, showing a great deal of the latter about the ears and tail.

They are quite mute, and very quiet in their movements...The nose is so good as to indicate the beagle descent, even if the head, tail and ears did not proclaim it. They are about 8 or 10lb in weight, and can hardly lift a full-sized hare. I have seen these dogs do more than any other retriever...'

John Henry Walsh, *The Pursuit of Wild Animals for Sport*, 1854

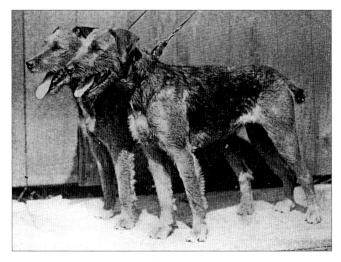

The harsh wiry coat of the 1905 Airedale.

Roger Free with his 14 inch Beagle and Terrier pack.

Sporting dogs earning their keep: *Coursing* **by Richard Ansdell, 1815–85.** (Charwynne Dog Features)

Shoulders difficult to judge in parti-dogs.
(Charwynne Dog Features)

LEFT: **Superb shoulders on a coursing greyhound.**

BELOW: **Greyhounds came to us from a function.**

SHOULDERING RESPONSIBILITY

In a recent letter to *Dog World*, lurcher expert Jackie Drakeford quite rightly corrected the words of a contributing vet-author by stating: 'Any working-bred hound or terrier will show how far forward the forelimbs need to be set, and there is never a 'ship's prow' chest in a true working dog... Anyone who has ever seen a running dog tight on the tail of hare, fox, rabbit or deer would know just how well they can twist and turn with those long backs and forelimbs set for forward reach.' Those valuable words sum up so succinctly the importance of the front assembly in lurchers. The power will always come from the back, but the manoeuvrability comes from the front.

If you study the writings and in particular the video made by the late Ronnie Wallace of hunting field fame, then you soon realise the importance to the hound of good shoulders. The video, *Hound Standards* (Countryside Audio and Visual), covers the conformation of the various hounds of the pack; it should be required listening for any show judge. Ronnie Wallace, the presenter, was chairman of the Master of Foxhounds Association for 22 years and hunted nine different packs of hounds. His writings too have been published in *A Manual of Foxhunting*, edited by Michael Clayton. Ronnie Wallace's genius as a hound breeder and his extraordinary achievements as a Master of Foxhounds made him a legend in his own lifetime. He should be listened to.

Wallace's advice on judging hounds is illuminating; he considers the shoulders the key to sound construction. Another famous hunting man, the late Sir Newton Rycroft, once wrote of a superb Beagle, Old Berkeley Rompish '39, in the hunting field '...she went past the whole pack to take the lead as a thoroughbred would outclass vanners. She was one of the smallest bitches in kennel but the only one with perfect shoulders.' Wallace and Rycroft were the great hound experts of the 20th century, their words are of immense value. Every show ring judge *must* judge shoulders with a knowledgeable eye. Winning hounds get bred from!

Expressions like 'lay of shoulder', 'well-laid shoulders' and 'sloping shoulders' are used by many without any clear concept of their implications, and, more important, the *reason* for their inclusion. Tom Horner, the great terrier judge, wrote extensively on this very point. His words are of value to judges of hounds and should never be scoffed at because they have been written by a terrier expert.

In his informative *All About The Bull Terrier* of 1973 (Pelham Books), Horner wrote: '...to secure the very important good lay back of shoulders, it is necessary for the dorsal bones to be of good length. Well laid back shoulders are highly desirable for a number of reasons, a well laid shoulder has a firmer attachment to the chest wall than an upright one, it is also likely to be matched by a good length of upper arm, which, in turn, will mean that the elbow will be placed well back from the forechest, and the foreleg will have freedom to reach out well in movement.' The stilted abbreviated front movement of so many show ring terrier breeds illustrates the limitation imposed on a dog's forward movement by a lack of slope in the shoulders and a lack of length in the upper arm.

It is easier to judge the shoulders of a short-coated self-coloured exhibit than any other. In a particoloured dog the patches on the shoulder can affect the way the human eye accepts the symmetry of the dog. On a black merle lurcher, for example, a solid black patch over the whole shoulder contrasts memorably with mainly white legs and a lighter-covered body; this can 'throw' the eye of the beholder and affect judgement.

For me, the first point of real quality in a dog lies in clean sloping shoulders. Well-placed shoulders give a perfect base for a proud head carriage. They provide too the balance between the length of the neck and the length of the back, preventing those disagreeable dips in topline which mar the whole appearance of a dog. I have learnt, over the years, to start any judgement of the shoulders by considering the position of the elbow. If the elbow is too far forward, then the dog is pulling itself along, not pushing itself along, not capitalising on the drive from the hocks, thighs and loins. In his video on the packhounds, Captain Wallace states that the shoulders are controlled by the elbow. He is worth heeding.

It is only when the scapula and the humerus are of the right length *and* correctly placed that a dog can achieve the desired length of stride and freedom in his front action. Sighthounds can have their upper arms 20% longer than their scapulae. In smaller breeds they tend to be equal in length. Dogs which step short in front are nearly always handicapped by upright shoulders and short steep upper arms. A dog of quality must have sloping shoulders and compatible upper arms to produce a good length of neck, a firm topline without dips, the right length of back and free movement on the forehand. Even when there is a discernible curve in the topline, as in the Borzoi and the Bedlington Terrier, well laid shoulders are required to produce the correct topline, with the arch in the spine starting in the correct place. The correct Borzoi and Bedlington 'arch' position is over the loins, to enable the dog to bring its hindfeet forwards, in front of the chest when galloping, without any restriction from the ribs.

When judging 'galloping breeds' I always check the space between their shoulder blades at the withers. If you check this space, say, to compare a show Greyhound with a coursing dog, by placing a finger between the two scapulae and then getting the dog to lower its head, you can soon spot the difference. The show dog's scapulae will squeeze your finger as the dog's head goes down; the coursing dog's scapulae will remain apart. In extreme cases this means that the show specimen would be quite unable to pick up a rabbit or even drink from a bowl on the floor, without adjusting its forelimbs. It is not good sense for the Greyhound's standard to demand shoulders that are 'narrow and cleanly defined at the top'; this can create a difficulty when the dog lowers its head.

The racing front involves an extremely long upper arm, often dropping the elbow below the brisket line. I have heard show judges declare this feature to be undesirable, even 'shelly'. But most of the desert Salukis I have seen hunt with great success possessed this feature, as do many quality lurchers. In the Dachshund front, the whole forehand structure is reduced in length of bones; the elbow action arc being actually above the brisket line. Many dogs which are loose at elbow are tight at the shoulder joint, the forelegs tending to be thrown out sideways in a circular movement. If the dog is tight at elbow the whole leg inclines outwards, making the dog 'paddle', i.e. move the feet in an arc to the side. Loose elbows are often accompanied by other front leg faults: slack pasterns, splayed feet or feet which turn in or out. Dogs with correctly sloping shoulders and compatible upper arms rarely have such a problem.

When shoulders are correctly sloped, the topline runs through much more smoothly, giving a far cleaner look. The shortening of the neck from the forward placement of the shoulders does seriously impede a working dog. A retriever, for example, with such a feature has to make so much more effort to pick up game or carry it over an obstacle or when swimming with it. Short-necked dogs tire far more quickly than soundly constructed ones. A few years ago, when making a commercial video on the Labrador Retriever, we were filming on the Sandringham estate and it was a joy to see the quite beautiful necks and shoulders of the sleek very fast black Labs which we filmed. No working dog deserves incompetent breeding bestowing handicapping features on it. When moving, 60 to 70% of a dog's weight is distributed on the front legs; the forequarter construction decides the soundness of the dog's movement.

Tom Horner wrote that 'Long-arched necks give flexibility to the head carriage and usually go along with good shoulder placement, the two combining to give the dog an air of quality and style.' Long cervical bones, long dorsal bones, a 'bump in the front', adequate upper arm length and a gap between the scapulae at the withers are not difficult to detect when viewing and 'going over' an exhibit. R H Smythe,

Lurcher with muscled shoulders. (Charwynne Dog Features)

Powerful shoulders: the greyhound of 1866 from Stonehenge's _The Dog of 1867_. (Charwynne Dog Features)

BELOW: **Sighthound physique essential.** (Charwynne Dog Features)

sportsman, vet, writer and exhibitor, once owned a brace of highly successful show Greyhounds, both over 27 inches' in height which could outrace a hare but never catch one. He also had a coursing Greyhound, 25 inches high, with 2½ fingers' width between the blade-bones, which once picked up 57 rabbits in three hours 'lamping' in similar country. The show Greyhounds were handicapped dogs, in the physical sense.

A famous Newmarket trainer used to stress 'No shoulder, no horse!' A famous professional huntsman once advised 'Necks and shoulders! get the necks and shoulders and the rest will come!' These are the cries needed for soundly built dogs; we select the breeding stock, so we shoulder the blame. Before we talk 'stud fee', let me see, and place hands on, your dog's shoulders! Let's shoulder responsibility rather than blame.

POSH LURCHER
All three need good shoulders to perform.
Attributed to John Duvall (1816–92)

Falconers 1887 Heywood-Hardy & Varley.
Salukis with falconer, 1887.

'The characteristics that set the Saluki complex (i.e. this type of sighthound, DH) apart from the true herding and working breeds was their independence and ability to work without human intervention. They are all "coursing" hounds, whatever their prey. A coursing hound is distinguished from the other hounds by several characteristics. First of all, they are built to run long distances at great speed. Secondly, they have enough length of muzzle to grab and hold prey, either by the leg or by the throat. Thirdly, they rely on their remarkable eyesight to course the prey, never taking their eyes off the target animal. Of course, they come equipped with noses, too, and they use them!'

Ann Chamberlain in her *Saluki*, Interpet Publishing, 2001.

A Lurcher with Dead Game in a Landscape 1819 James Berenger.
Sheer speed never enough.

'With respect to the lurcher, it appears to us to be a mongrel breed between the rough greyhound and the shepherd's dog. Bewick, who figures and describes it, says, that it is less and shorter than the greyhound, with stronger limbs; its body is covered with a coat of rough hair, commonly of a pale yellow colour; its aspect is sullen, and its habits, whence it derives its name, are cunning and insidious. At the same time it must be confessed that this dog is very attached to its master, displays most extraordinary intelligence, and is trained with great facility. As it possesses the advantage of a fine scent, it is often nefariously employed during the night-time in the capture of game; the more especially as it works silently, never giving tongue.'

WCL Martin in his *The History of the Dog*, Charles Knight, 1845.

Lurcher with a Dead Fox 1777 Stephen Elmer ARA 1717-96.

Quality lies in performance.

'With respect to the lurcher… When taken to the warren, it steals along with the utmost caution, creeps upon the rabbits while feeding, and darts upon them in an instant; it waylays them as they return to their burrow, where it is ready to seize them, and then brings its booty to its master. Bewick knew a man who kept a pair of these dogs, and who confessed that at any time he could procure in an evening as many rabbits as he could carry home. This dog is equally expert at taking hares, partly by speed, but more by cunning wiles. It will drive partridges to the net with the utmost circumspection and address; and will even seize and pull down a fallow deer, and, leaving it disabled, return to its master and guide him to the scene of its exploits. The true lurcher is not so often to be seen as formerly; it is essentially a poacher's dog, so that any person known to possess one becomes a suspected character.'

WCL Martin in his *The History of the Dog*, Charles Knight, 1845.

The Waterloo Cup Meeting 1840 Richard Ansdell 1815-85.

'All coursing men pay particular attention to depth of chest, quality of back and **loins**, and still more to the hindquarters – i.e. the rump, the first and second thighs as well as the hock joints and pasterns. It is almost impossible to be too insistent regarding highly developed muscles and broad loins, where so much action is brought into play when a Greyhound is running and twisting after the hare.'

Frank Townend Barton MRCVS in his *Our Dogs*, Jarrolds, 1938.

Dodger Wilson Hepple 1854–1937.

'Dodger' was a red dog by 'Fugitive' out of 'Ellen Johnson', whelped in 1879. He won the Waterloo Plate, the consolation stake for dogs beaten in the second round of the Waterloo Cup, in February 1881. He also divided the final of a major stake at Gosforth Park (an enclosed coursing ground on Newcastle racecourse) and later stood as a stud dog. He was the property of the prominent Northumberland owner Mr N Dunn, and sometimes ran in the nomination of his friend 'Captain Ellis' a pseudonym for the vicar of Bothal, Northumberland.

Mariner, winner of Swaffham Cup 1834 RW Folkard/Pinx 1834.

'Speaking in an Irish kind of manner, a Greyhound is no Greyhound if it is not kept in constant training; both heart, lungs and muscular system must be maintained in the highest standard of vigour. If exercise is insufficient or irregularly given the muscles become soft, the heart becomes weak, and its power to respond to increased exertion fails; being a hollow muscular organ, there is a tendency for its fibres to degenerate when thrown into a state of comparative ease. When the muscles covering the skeleton are manipulated they should convey the sensation of being hard as boards, and the outlines of the individual muscles be plainly discernible; and the more vigorous the exercise, provided such is carried out with regularity, the better the muscular development.'

Frank Townend Barton MRCVS in his *Hounds*, Long, 1913.

Poachers Deerstalking Sir Edwin Henry Landseer RA.
Scale of Poaching.

Historically poaching was conducted on a large scale. The poaching gang operating in the New Forest in the 1620s was over fifty strong. In Yorkshire in 1640, a poaching gang of around forty, killed over seventy deer in Wortley Park. The infamous Russell gang of 1619 ranged over four counties, carrying away 327 red and fallow deer, 1,000 hares, 1,400 rabbits, 5,000 pheasants and 1,000 partridges.

(Charwynne Dog Features)

Le Maitre d'equipage negre Jean Leon Gerome 1854.

'In the show rings of the United States, the sighthound breeds appear to be losing breed-type in the pursuit of a generalised "sighthound" phenotype, arising from the seeking of 'TRAD' – tremendous reach and drive. This is resulting in overlong vertical necks, set at a strange angle to the shoulders, shallow croups and over-angulation in the stifle. In time, in the exhibition world there, the functional sighthound will disappear, as the desire for a statuesque exhibit imposes a false stance-led type which could not function as a sporting dog.'

LEARNING ABOUT LOINS

Over many years of dog-owning, the greatest joy for me has been to see my dogs galloping, really stretching their legs. I marvel at their remarkable physical coordination as well as savouring their spiritual release. Writer after writer will tell you of 'the powerhouse of the hindquarters' and the importance of the correct amount of bend in the stifle. Not so many will extol the extraordinary balance, synchronised control and anatomical harmony behind such athleticism. The powerhouse of the hindquarters cannot be harnessed if the flexibility of the spine and the transmission of power isn't there too. The link between the fore and hindquarters of the running dog captures the strength of the dog, but it's a link not always appreciated.

'To acquire the perfect silhouette the dog must obviously have sufficient length of loin to avoid the cramped, wheel-back stance which has periodically been quite common. This extra bit of loin is what makes the dog cover a lot of ground and was what Mrs McKay at the Laguna kennels always impressed on me made all the difference between an ordinary whippet and a top-class one.' Those words from Bo Bengtson's book on the Whippet represent surprisingly rare coverage of this vital part of a dog's anatomy. Whole chapters have been written on heads and page after page on shoulders; a number of books are devoted to coat colour alone; but the loin is sadly neglected, usually only given a passing reference by sporting authors too. This is both an alarming omission and not a good omen for the breeding of soundly constructed dogs.

But what is the loin? The Kennel Club definition describes it as the 'Region of the body on either side of the vertebral column between the last ribs and hindquarters'. From that brief imprecise description, it is easy and forgiveable to understate the importance of this part of the canine anatomy. Nearly every breed standard dismisses the loin in a few words; it is rare to read even a mention of the loin in judges's critiques of their show entry. This might be understandable in say a Toy breed, but is a disappointing oversight in hound, terrier or gundog breeds. When I watch judges going over exhibits at shows I am amazed at how little attention is paid to this desperately important part of the canine anatomy.

It is not unusual for those involved in dogs to be fairly hazy about the loin. I can recall standing ringside at a hound show, with a distinguished judge, and listening to his observations, especially those based on his confusing the hounds' flanks with their loins! A much-respected lurcher breeder once told me that for years he had thought that the groin was another word for the loin. I once sat through a two-hour lecture on locomotion in the dog, given by a lecturer from a vet school, and realised that the loin had not been mentioned once. He did refer to muscles like the rectus abdominis, the principal flexor of the spine, the great oblique, which arches the back, flexes the spine or inclines it laterally, and the lumbo-dorsal/thoracolumbar fascia, where the loin is situated.

This distinguished scientist was so used to lecturing to students, undergraduates with a good knowledge of anatomy, that he had forgotten the importance of respectful simplification to an audience which lacked specialist knowledge but contained people just as intelligent, and certainly more perceptive, than he. What he lacked the empathy to explain was that the loins comprise the lumbar area, extending from the end of the ribcage to the start of the pelvis, forming the upper section of the couplings region. The coupling comprises the whole muscular band joining the chest and hindquarters, not just in the loin area. The loins overlie the lumbar vertebrae, can differ in length, flexibility and capability, according to the length of these bones and their substance, as well as to the width of their prominence on each side. This accounts for breed differences, originating in function.

No breed wants sagging loins, giving a drooping backline at the coupling. But requirements vary in breeds from slightly tucked loins, arched loins and a need to be 'light in loins'. The American Kennel Club standard for the American Staffordshire Terrier calls for 'loins slightly tucked'. This demands a waisted appearance from above or a dog 'slightly drawn in loins'. Our standard for the Dachshund expects a slightly arched loin which is short and strong, predictably in such a long-backed breed. The Basenji is expected to feature a short-coupled loin, with a definite waist, perhaps confusing the coupling with the loin. Most Staffordshire Bull Terriers that I see are light in loin, perhaps out of a desire to produce the appreciable waist in an otherwise muscular breed. The loin is not mentioned however in this breed standard.

The loin has the same function and location in every breed. Judges of each breed need to be aware of the loin. Good length of loin can make a dog look more rectangular than square, when the actual distance from the sternum to the point of buttock is in reality not much greater than the height at the withers. A short-loined exhibit can so often be more eye-catching, especially if it displays a long neck and upright shoulders, but it is not a sound animal.

The long dorsal muscle, which extends the spine or bends it to one side, is especially noticeable in the loins, where each vertebral bone carries the weight of the body in front of it, together with the weight of its own body mass. Towards the sacrum, each vertebra is accepting greater total weight than the one before it – the vertebrae enlarge, moving rearwards, throughout the lumbar region. It is not difficult to appreciate therefore the importance to the huge heavy dog, as well as the fast lithe leaping dog, of the loin. Breeders of Foxhounds have long been aware of this importance.

Captain Ronnie Wallace, perhaps the most respected hound breeder of the 20th century, has written on this subject: 'It is very nice to see a back bone set in two cushions of muscle so that you could roll a billiard ball down it with no difficulty...you can have either a straight back, or the arched loins known as 'wheel backs'. Either of these may be acceptable, but you must have the right equipment at the back to go with them.' He is stressing the mutual support needed between the loins and the hindlimbs. Richard Clapham, the Fell Hound expert, stressed this too, pointing out that the muscles of the loin are connected to those of the hindlegs, so that any weakening of the former lessens the hound's ability to use his hindleg muscles efficiently.

Fifty years ago, Clapham wrote: 'The longer the body, the greater is the call upon certain muscles such as the broad dorsal muscle, which begins below the shoulder and spreads over the back and sides of the chest, until it tapers towards the loin. With increased length of loin, the hound is unable to get his hind legs well under his body, and the internal organs being spread over greater length, the strain in a downward direction is likewise increased. Thus, unless the muscles of the big hound are abnormally developed, he suffers from loss of power and endurance.' The latter is a vital point; hound breeders acknowledged the impact made by sagging loins on endurance, but also knew the limitations of the hound being *too* short-coupled. Generally speaking, over-shortness of body, as opposed to shortness of back, carries more disadvantages than a little extra length, which gives more flexibility and easier whelping. A good Bull Terrier demonstrates this point well.

The flexibility needed when say a Greyhound is racing is quite astounding: the hind feet 'overtake' the fore feet, with the loin and the thigh both curved into just about a semi-circle when the hindlimb is stretched forward to its very limit. The elasticity which permits this is astonishing, but the soundness of construction and muscularity of the dog allows it. The loins have no support at all from any bones other than the seven lumbar vertebrae and act as the crucial link, the keystone 'bridge', between the front limbs, from the ribs forward, and the rear limbs – the legs, pelvis and tail. For structural strength, a slight arch here is essential, but too great an arch is a weakness. That is why the gift of 'an eye for a dog' puts one judge in a different class from another. A desirable arched loin can be confused with a roach or sway back.

Lurcher with good arched loins.

Long-loined lurcher. (Charwynne Dog Features)

Strong (on the near dog) loins and weak loins (on the far dog)

MUSCLES OF THE LOINS

'It is by the propulsatory efforts of the muscles of the loins and thighs that progression is so much accelerated in this race; and wherever the muscular markings are meagre, the killing properties are small; we therefore recommend every sportsman to avoid breeding from any such defective proportions.' Delabere Blaine, *An Encyclopaedia of Rural Sports*, Longman, 1870

Victorian greyhounds with powerful loins.

Below: **Even the thick coat doesn't conceal the powerful loin: Miss A Doxford's Highland Deerhound Ch Noel of Ruritania, depicted in 1925.**

The strength of loin very apparent: Miss F A White's coursing greyhound Ch Fascinating Ways, depicted in 1925.

A dog may get away with a sagging loin in the show ring or even on the flags at a hound show; but it would never do so as a working or sporting dog. It would lack endurance and would suffer in old age. Yet it is, for me, comparatively rare to witness a judge in any ring in any breed test the scope, muscularity and hardness of the loin through a hands-on examination. For such a vital part of the dog's anatomy to go unjudged is a travesty. It doesn't take much imagination to appreciate the supreme importance of the loins to the speedsters, the sighthound breeds. Some Greyhound experts have argued that the muscular development of the back is probably the most important single factor in the anatomical construction of the Greyhound, ahead of the muscular hindquarters.

Down the centuries, the words have been consistent: Berners – 'Backed lyke a beam'; Markham – 'A square and flat back, short and strong fillets'; Cox – 'Arched, broad, supple and showing enormous muscular development'; Stonehenge – 'The loins must therefore be broad, strong and deep, and the measure of their strength must be a circular one'. In his informative book on the greyhound, H Edwards Clarke writes: 'The very first test that any trainer makes of the condition of a greyhound is to run his hand over its back and loins... The first impression by touch should be one of supple firmness, of well-developed muscular tissue of a rubber-like consistency.' Like Capt Wallace he sought a little trough or valley along the backbone. He looked for arching of muscle not any arching of the skeleton, a common fault in our show sighthounds, especially in Whippets and Borzois.

Clarke termed the roach or 'camel' back a skeletal malformation, a form of spinal curvature that 'mili-

tates against any possibility of smooth-flowing, free-striding movement'. At a championship show a few years ago, I saw a lady exhibitor proudly posing her winning Greyhound for the dog-press photographers despite its very obvious camel back! The somewhat brief breed standard for the Greyhound stresses an arched loin both in the General Appearance and the Body sections; perhaps a few more words on the need for a muscular arch rather than a skeletal arch would be a better guide. The standard of the Borzoi actually demands a back that is bony, free from any cavity and rising in a curve.

The Whippet is expected to feature a definite arch over its loin; the Borzoi however is supposed to possess the highest point of the curve in its back over the last rib, i.e. forward of the loin. Both are sighthounds built for speed. The American standard for the Borzoi calls for a back which is 'rising a little at the loins in a graceful curve'. That is more than a little different from ours and more likely to produce an efficient sighthound. There is a world of difference between a bent skeleton over the last rib and a curve of muscle over the loins, the latter benefiting the dog! The lumbar vertebrae are quite literally the backbones of the loins, lumbus being Latin for loin. Any arch should be over the lumbar vertebrae and not further forward.

In an attempt to appreciate the value of the loin to the dog, I think of the dog as a four-wheel drive rear-engined vehicle with its transmission in the loins. They are an absolutely key feature of the canine anatomy relating to movement. If we prize movement then we must understand the loins. But just try researching the subject even in weighty books on dogs. It is vitally important for any real lurcher man to learn about loins.

Coursing Needs

All coursing men pay particular attention to depth of chest, quality of back and *loins*, and still more to the hindquarters – i.e. the rump, the first and second thighs as well as the hock joints and pasterns. It is almost impossible to be too insistent regarding highly developed muscles and broad loins, where so much action is brought into play when a greyhound is running and twisting after the hare.

Frank Townend Barton MRCVS, *Our Dogs*, Jarrolds, 1938

Arab with Saluki. (Charles Hamilton, 1862, Charwynne Dog Features)

**Rough-haired Ibizan Hound of 1904:
much more lurcher-like and less
refined.**
(Charwynne Dog Features)

CHAPTER 5

LURCHER SKILLS OVERSEAS

Hunting in India involved all kinds of strong hounds – bred for pace and persistence.

Below: **Note the powerful brindle gazehound, possibly a Shenkottah hound from the Trivandrum District, a big game hunting ground, once used in the tiger hunt.**

RAMPUR HOUND
Indian lurcher. The hunting dogs of the nomadic Indian peoples today fall into two types: the lighter-boned smooth-coated Mudhol or Karvani dogs and the stronger-boned silky feathered Pashmi or Pisouris, which can range from 20 to 28 inches. They are used on a wide variety of quarry, from chinkara and blackbuck, fox and rabbit to civet and mongoose, even black-faced monkeys, a local pest.

LURCHERS OF THE DESERT

Find a desert and a sighthound will not be far away. For a hound which hunts by speed and capitalises on superb eyesight, the desert is the hunting ground to excel in. The Saluki, the Sloughi, the Awazakh and the I-Twini much further south all exploit their remarkable sprinting ability and capability to detect animal movement at long range. They are pot-fillers where other predators do not succeed; they are canine hunters where other sporting dogs cannot hunt. Only the cheetah rivals their success, with perhaps the Abyssinian wolf a contender. The Saluki is easily the best known desert sighthound, with the feathered variety well established in Europe. Commendably, some of the Saluki owners in Britain have coursed their hounds and now use them for lure-chasing.

There is no single type of Saluki. Most of the hounds I've seen in middle eastern countries have been smooth-haired (the Nejdi type), not feathered (the Shami or Syrian type). The smooth coat is dominant. In the pedigree world we have smooth and feathered hounds registered as Salukis, with the smooth-coated Sloughi (from North Africa) listed as a separate breed. The Arabs there however referred to them as mogrebi or western. The Tuareg Sloughi, sometimes known as the 'oska', is classified separately in some countries as the Azawakh Sloughi, from the valley of that name in Mali and Niger. Both the Azawakh and the Sloughi have been found to possess an additional allele on the glucose phosphate isomerase gene locus, not found in other sighthounds but also featuring in the jackal, suggesting a separate origin. Circassia, in the Caucasus, was once famous for its sighthounds; but Circassians can be found in Syria, Iraq, Jordan and Turkey too. The Shilluk Greyhound from the plains of the White Nile in Southern Sudan is more Saluki-like than Greyhound-like. The Poligar and the Vaghari of India too have a distinct smooth Saluki look to them.

The deserts of the Indian sub-continent have proved good hunting grounds for sighthounds. The Sindh Hound is found in the deserts of Sindh and Rajasthan and famous as a boar-lurcher, being Great Dane size: 28 to 30 inches and around 100lb in weight. Lighter and more Sloughi-like is the Rampur Hound, the Greyhound of Northern India, the Maharajah of Baria once having a famous kennel. Around 28 inches at the shoulder and weighing around 75lb, they have been used on stag and boar and for hunting jackal. A century ago, some were brought to Britain and exhibited at the Dublin show. The lurcher of Maharashtra is the Mudhol Hound, between the Greyhound and the Whippet in size. More Saluki-like is the lurcher of the Banjara, a nomadic tribe with gypsy conections. The Banjara, or Vanjari, is famed for its stamina and nose and its ability to pull down deer, always going for the hindquarters, not the throat, as many Deerhounds do instinctively.

The Chippiparai, the lurcher of the south, is described as being Dobermann-like in outline, but usually white in colour and used mainly for hare-hunting. They are regarded as the most intelligent and biddable Indian breed, being used as police dogs in some areas. The Poligar Hound is the Greyhound of Southern India; they have been called the lurcher of India, used on fox, deer, jackal, and, in packs, on boar. For generations this breed was used for pig-hunting on foot with spears, rather as the ancient Greeks hunted them. Around 26 inches at the shoulder and weighing between 40 and 45lb, they are thin-coated but the coat has a stiff wiry texture, harsh to the hand when back-brushed. They are famous long-distance runners but sadly for a delicate constitution, needing careful rearing.

In a different continent and of a totally different type are the tribal dogs of South Africa. This remarkable group of dogs has been researched and then publicised by Johan Gallant in South Africa, after centuries of European indifference. Any group of dogs which can survive without ever receiving any veterinary care, in a testing climate like the South African bush and operating in terrain which would challenge any functional animal, deserves attention. The Africanis is believed to be a direct descendant of the domestic dogs which came to southern Africa with the Iron Age migrations of the Bantu-speaking people. These dogs were then taken up by the resident Khoisan people; these dogs were never bred for type but type developed from function.

Natural selection has not only eliminated inheritable diseases and provided a natural resistance to internal and external parasites, it has created a virile, healthy, functionally excellent animal, repeating the formula applied automatically by primitive dog breeders all over the world. It is only in the highly civilised countries where, paradoxically, sickly short-lived dogs are bred from because they are handsome or conform to a rigid blueprint. There is nothing exaggerated or extravagant in the Africanis; their coats adapt to the seasons, they move with great economy of movement and their owners have no obsession with ear carriage – their dogs can have drop ears or erect ones. These dogs have survived in a harsh setting and are genetically important.

The generic term Africanis embraces several types of dog; the I-Twina, now quite rare, is a living representative of the Iron Age dog, and a sighthound described as the original hunting dogs of the Xhosa. The I-Baku, big or floppy-eared in the Xhosa tongue, longer-haired and featuring a hind dew claw, is the long distance sighthound, unlike the I-Twina which is a sprinter. The I-Nqeqe, or I-Maku to Zulus, conforms to the same type, but has a blunter shorter muzzle. Some Europeans have noted a certain Border Collie look to these dogs, which are found across a wide area. The more streamlined I-Bansi are the most competent hunting dogs, able to hunt using sight and scent. The Zulus have their Sica dogs, which can vary in appearance, never having been subjected to selective breeding, and can be found right across the Zulu homeland.

Also from Africa come the Azawakhs, a breed that has lived for thousands of years with the nomadic tribesmen of the Berber and Tuareg. Azawakh means 'land of the north' and spans Niger and Mali. Unusually for a sighthound breed the Azawakh is also used as a herding dog and watchdog. If the Sloughi is the Arabian sighthound, then the Azawakh is the African one. Their temperament is alleged to be more feline than canine, perhaps from their natural aloofness and independence of mind. Looking taller than the other sighthound breeds, they have thin skins, a prominent sternum and very deep chest and a very high tuck-up, making some look almost skeletal. Body ratios are considered important in this breed: height of chest/height at withers = about 4:10, length of muzzle/length of head = 1:2 and width of skull/length of head = 4:10. It is often confused with the Sloughi, especially the desert type in this breed, the mountain type of Sloughi being taller and more robust.

The desert sighthounds are true lurchers; most are unrecognised and unregistered, but they have been carefully bred to function. They should never be underestimated as highly effective hunting dogs, surviving hard times in tough places.

'It is of course possible that the Saluqi of times past was used in a much wider role than is customary today. In Central Asia for example it seems it is indeed a much more versatile hound using scent as well as sight to locate its prey. However in desert conditions there is not much scope for scenting game; whereas the open terrain is conducive to hunting by sight... It is a well-known phenomenon that faculties atrophy if they are not exercised. So it is just possible that in earlier times the Saluqi hunted both by scent and by sight.'

Terence Clark and Muawiya Derhalli, *Al-Mansur's Book On Hunting*, Aris & Phillips Ltd, 2001

'The Sahara Desert tribes call the Saluki Barake, or 'Specially Blessed'. Nowhere in North Africa or Arabia is the Saluki ever sold between tribes or members of tribes. He is always given as a present of honour either to an eminent guest or to a favoured friend. In the Libyan Desert the tribesmen speak of this graceful hound as el Hor, 'the Noble One', and they say of him as they say of their horses, 'are not these the herited of our fathers, and shall not we to our sons bequeath them?''

James Wentworth Day, *The Dog in Sport*, Harrap, 1938

Brindle and fawn African native hunting dogs. (Johan Gallant)

BELOW: **All types of strong-running hounds were used in the Indian hunt. Portrayed here are a rough-coated gazehound (i.e. a par force hound, not a sighthound) and a parti-coloured 'gazelle-lurcher'.**

Lt Col Walter Stirling with a Gazelle-Hound, Damascus 1917.

The Grecian Greyhound (Youatt)

Cirneco dell'Etna.
(Charwynne Dog Features)

The large Portuguese Hound (Portugues Podengo). By kind permission of the Portuguese Kennel Club
(Charwynne Dog Features)

LURCHERS OF THE
MEDITERRANEAN LITTORAL

Despite much holidaying there, British sportsmen seem to know little of the hunting dogs of the Mediterranean littoral. You are unlikely to find the blood of say an Ibizan Hound, a Sicilian Hound, a Portuguese Podengo or a Cretan Hound featuring in the lurcher blends of Britain. This is a loss, for these breeds are robust, breed true to type, have sound feet, good noses, lightning reactions to quarry and proven prowess on rabbit, a more difficult catch than many realise. These Mediterranean hounds hunt by sight and scent and cannot be pigeon-holed as either scent or sighthounds. This alone should attract the interest of lurcher men looking beyond outcrosses to pastoral breeds, however clever and biddable the latter may be. But as the range of quarry here is legally limited and rabbit or rat hunting easily available sport, a look at these all-round sporting dogs makes some sense.

The German scientist Max Hilsheimer links all these hounds to a common ancestor the Tesem, writing: 'This breed has died out in modern Egypt, but still exists in Crete, the Balearic Islands and Pityusa... The island of Ibiza is the chief breeding centre...' Long-time Ibizan Hound breeder, Rafael Serra of Vinebre near Catalunya in Spain, has written that: 'The Ibizan Hound is a farmer's hunting dog... which hunts rabbits in packs over rough rocky terrain, mainly at a ground-covering trot, but which needs repeated short bursts of speed involving extreme agility and high jumps.' There is, unusually for this type of hound, a rough-coated variant, believed to come from an outcross to hounds from further north. Ibizans will retrieve live game to hand, having soft mouths despite their sharp muzzles. They are distinctive, with their pink noses, large mobile ears, amber eyes and a wrinkled frown. They are renowned for their 'suspended trot', an effortless economical 'hover-stride', of value in a hot dusty energy-sapping terrain.

The Pharoah Hound, developed from the Kelb Tal-Fenek, the Rabbit Dog of Malta and Gozo, has yet to find a sporting use in Britain. They hunt by sight and scent, with the imported and now show-bred hounds being heavier and taller than the original Maltese hounds, which remain in a hunter's mould, leaner and finer in bone. A few years ago, a judge's show critique on this breed read: 'It is some years since I have judged my second breed, and sadly, what I have been told was unfortunately only too true. Breeders, what have you done to this lovely breed?... Briskets seem to be a thing of the past and so many with such an upright upper arm and no length of humerus, with resultant bad movement.' Once any sporting breed escapes from its given function, its breeders seem to get lost.

The Sicilian Hound or Cirneco dell'Etna is a little bat-eared hound used on rabbit in Sicily. Still very much a sporting breed, there are around three dozen in Britain at the moment, and any sportsman seeking a small active charming hound for lurcher-breeding would do well to look at this unspoiled breed. They have, back in Sicily, their own field trials, and, having been specifically bred for hunting terrain formed by volcanic lava, superb feet and great heat tolerance. Extremely hardy, they have excellent noses, having being described as scenthounds with a sighthound build. In their native country, they are renowned 'searchers', that is, famed for picking up air and ground scent at long distances, then advancing to use their acute eyesight to mark the presence of game. This breed, hardly known here, offers valuable breeding material.

The Sicilian hounds work to their own field trial regulations, covering shooting over game and trials without guns. Around 150 hounds are newly registered there each year. It is worth noting that their field trial regulations stipulate that: Dogs that do not make a tenacious effort in their work; that hesitate on a scent trail; that are distracted and do not cover the ground designated for their turn within the first five minutes will be eliminated. They are used to working with ferrets and at 46 to 50 cm (18 to 20 inches) lack the legginess of the 22 to 29 inch Ibizan Hound. Some have been imported, and registered with the KC, but not so far by sportsmen.

The Cretan Hound is rarely favoured outside its native country and island. There are around 1,000 in Crete itself and perhaps around 150 in mainland Greece, nearly all owned by hunters. They are used on hare and rabbit with the stamina to hunt for six to seven hours at 30 to 36 degrees celsius; they are lightly built but remarkably agile, coping better with their prey in rocky thorny terrain than on the plains. These hounds use scent and then sight when pursuing their quarry, which has to be dispatched with the gun, not caught by the hound, under Greek law. There is I understand a problem with temperament in the breed, which, commendably, is being faced and breeding plans geared to eradicating this feature. There once was a Greek sighthound, with a painting from 1835 depicting one, but they have long been extinct.

The Portuguese Hound or Podengo comes in three sizes, with the smallest making good ground in the show rings here. Yellow, tan or dark grey, with a smooth or rough coat, but thicker than most hound coats, they are extremely agile, bred to operate in rough cover, on stony ground, over terraced or hilly country. The Great Podengo may now be extinct and is Rhodesian Ridgeback-sized; the medium variety is harrier-like and used to hunt rabbit for the gun and in small packs; the small variety is used as an earth-dog and as a ratter on board boats. Remarkably bright and alert, the latter is now rapidly gaining ground in Britain and would make a sound outcross for too closely bred terrier lines here. They have stable temperaments and an uplifting chirpiness about them.

Not every lurcher expert has written to recommend these Mediterranean breeds however. Brian Plummer, in his *Secrets of Dog Training* (Robinson, 1992) stated: 'Not only do these hounds possess the rather remote disposition of the typical Middle Eastern sighthound, but they also have excellent olfactory senses and a tendency to run head down on the scent of game... In the hands of an experienced and competent trainer, the pharaoh hound and the Ibizan hound can be versatile and useful hunting dogs – in Malta and the Balearic Islands they occupy the same role as the lurcher in Britain – though they are infinitely more difficult to train... when I specialised in training recalcitrant sighthounds, owners of Ibizan and pharaoh hounds were the most frequent clients.'

Britons holidaying in the Canaries may under-rate the sporting potential there; but the Podencos Canarios, or hunting dogs, find plenty of sport on rabbit there, even in Lanzarote. This type of sporting dog is found too in Majorca, as well as Ibiza. The rabbits there don't live underground but in crevices, piles of rocks or in crumbling stone walls. As both the late Brian Plummer and Ted Walsh frequently pointed out, catching rabbits above ground is never easy. They may be classed as vermin and sneered at by the more privileged hunter but they can make a good hare-dog look stupid. The Sicilians pride their rabbit-dog, the Cirneco dell'Etna, on its scenting skill just as much as its speed and agility. Hounds bred for rabbit seem to be brighter and more versatile than many others, perhaps because the rabbit is deceptively testing prey. Ibizan Hounds would be better in open ground, Greek Hounds, Portuguese Podengos and Cirnechi dell'Etna in hedgerows, quarries, deserted mines or abandoned industrial sites. Diversify your gene-pool!

Do we not need formal trials for lurchers like those for the Sicilian Hounds? Do we rely far too much on infusions of sheepdog blood in our lurcher blends? Why use pastoral dog characteristics in a hunting dog when there are hounds which can supply the cleverness, response to training and field directions and the alertness desired in a lurcher? The endless debates about the relative merits of Beardie, Border Collie or even Pyrenean Sheepdog blood will endure. But a long look at the Sicilian Hound would be worthwhile. These handy-sized lively biddable clever little hunting dogs deserve more than a passing glance from lurcher-men. There is not much 'genetic junk' in these long-proven robust extremely agile very alert hyperactive hounds, unlike some recently imported stock. Where they come from, incompetent hunting dogs or sickly mutts just aren't bred from.

'When hunting young animals, gazelle for example, the tjesm could probably kill outright, by breaking the quarry's neck, as some modern hounds are able to do. This is suggested on the Hemaka disc, where the black hound has a gazelle by the throat. In pursuit of small game such as hare the tjesm would have been unbeatable, for it doubtless shared the remarkable ability of greyhounds and that of its modern counterparts to 'lock on' to the quarry and instantly to replicate its movements, no matter how energetically the prey attempts to shake off its pursuer.'

Michael Rice, *Swifter than the Arrow, The Golden Hunting Hounds of Ancient Egypt*, Taurus, 2006

Bat-eared sighthounds are found all around the Mediterranean. (Charwynne Dog Features)

RIGHT: **Kritikos Lagonikos or Cretan Hound.** (Charwynne Dog Features)

Pharoah Hound.

Borzoi racing, Germany 1966.

Circassian Borzoi. (Charwynne Dog Features)

Chortaj. (Charwynne Dog Features)

LURCHERS OF THE STEPPES

When lamenting the misguided contemptible class-warfare behind the malicious Hunting with Dogs Act, which now denies many a working class sportsman his chance to fill his family's cooking pot, it is easy to overlook the previous prohibition of coursing large and small game with sighthounds on mainland Europe: in France in 1844, in Germany in 1848 and in Holland in 1924. Before this legislation, northern Europe had a distinguished heritage of hunting with sighthounds: levriers in France, windhunden in Germany and the rough and smooth-coated Friese Windhond of the Netherlands. The Chart Polski or Polish Greyhound and the Magyar Agar or Hungarian Greyhound are still with us and the new meritocracy in Russia seems to be reviving the hunting Borzoi. We know little of the Chortaj or West Russian Coursing Hound or Eastern Greyhound and the Steppe Borzoi or South Russian Steppe Hound, both smooth-coated 26 inch sighthounds.

The longer-haired Russian Wolfhound or Borzoi, championed by the Tsars and lionised by writers such as Turgenev and Tolstoi, was patronised here initially by the nobility and has maintained popularity without finding a field use. I did once learn of one being used, devastatingly, on fox in Scotland however. Behind the modern single breed of Russian Borzoi, there are barrel-chested Caucasian Borzoi, huge curly-haired Courtland Borzoi and bigger-boned Crimean dogs. This type was found as far west as Albania too. The Kennel Club Borzoi is now confined by a closed gene pool, in the rigid pusuit of purity rather than performance, but the lesser known Borzoi types are really South Russian lurchers both in employment and in breeding method. Hungry peasants and level-headed kulaks didn't keep hounds because they were pretty!

The real all-round 'hunting by speed' field dogs from Russia are the mid-Asiatic Tasy or East Russian Coursing Hound and the Taigan or Kirghiz Borzoi.

The Circassian Greyhound, also known as the Crimean, Caucasian or Tartary Greyhound, is more Saluki-like, understandably so, as the Circassians could be found as far afield as Syria and Iraq.

The Tasy and the Taigon, both over two feet at the withers, are fast, robust, determined, all-purpose hunting dogs and like the similar breeds of Chortaj (pronounced Hortai) and the Steppe Borzoi, remain unrecognised by most international registries. This means that their breeding remains in the hands of the hunters not the exhibitors. The Tasy hails from the desert plains east of the Caspian Sea, featuring a ringed tail and heavy ear feathering, with a likely common origin with the better known Afghan Hound, sometimes called the Tazi in its native country. Used on hare, fox, marmot, hoofed quarry and even wolf, the Tasy is remarkably agile, with a good nose as well as great speed and legendary stamina, often being used with the hawk, providing fur pelts as well as meat. One famous Tasy was valued at 47 horses, such was its prowess in the hunt.

The Taigon operated further east, in the high altitude Tien Shan region on the border with China. Used, sometimes with falcons, to hunt fox, marmot, badger, hare, wildcat, wolf and hoofed game, these sighthounds could follow scent too but were renowned for their extraordinary stamina at high altitude. They may disappear as more urban living consumes their fanciers but their blood could be so valuable to the inbred pedigree sighthounds of the west. But of course, breed purity comes ahead of performance in today's canine agenda, despite the health dangers of close inbreeding for over a century.

Further south, the time-honoured Cossack tradition of coursing is conducted on the vast steppes from the north Caucasus, west of the Caspian, up through the Volga and Don River estuaries, where abundant game is available, and the Chortaj and the Steppe Borzoi excel. The mounted hunters use a

Tasy. (Charwynne Dog Features)

BELOW: **Taigan.**

HUNTING WITH HAWK AND HOUND
Charles Hamilton (exh 1831–67) *An Arab horseman holding a falcon.*

brace of sighthounds and a falcon instead of a gun, a style taken further west by the Tartars. Neither breed has achieved registration and this has permitted the best hunting dogs to be used as breeding material rather than the prettiest poseur in the ring. These hounds are prized for what they can do, once the only test for any sporting dog. The steppe sighthounds are famed for their ability to sprint over huge distances, for their remarkable eyesight and for being able to show great speed at the end of a lung-bursting long chase. Not surprisingly, they possess supremely tough feet.

These South Russian lurchers, for that is what they are, have never known food manufactured just for dogs, have never experienced veterinary care and have always been bred for hunting performance; their survival indicates their anatomical soundness and physical robustness and they represent a unique gene pool, a source for good both from a sporting and a health point of view. As we increasingly impose our moral vanity on the under-developed world and show increasing disrespect to unsophisticated hunters, whether they are seeking fur clothing or food for their table, merely to survive, we need to take stock.

'The Crimean Greyhound has pendant ears, which would seem to denote an entirely different origin from the English Greyhound. Whatever may have been the exact origin of the Russian Borzoi, the ancient type of this hound has little except speed lines which would make it show any blood relationship to the other breeds, and the subdivisions or variations differ but little one from the other. To summarise, hounds of this ancient type, which existed in all purity in Russia previous to the beginning of the nineteenth century, had little or no stop to the skull, tremendous depth of chest, were rather flat-sided, and had great length of tail, the hair of which in frequent instances trailed on the ground. The coat was long and silky.'

Joseph Thomas, *Observations on Borzoi*, Houghton Mifflin, 1912

Perchino Borzois. (Charwynne Dog Features)

Cross-bred Wolfhounds, North Dakota, 1908.
(Charwynne Dog Features)

COURSING ON THE PLAINS
History will never tell who
was the first American to see a
jack-rabbit. Whoever it was,
he must have instantly felt the
need of a Greyhound. This
large hare of the Western
plains has a dash of speed
which takes him quickly out
of the range of any ordinary
dog, and an endurance which
precludes the idea of being
captured by any plan which
involves his stopping from
exhaustion ahead of a slow
pursuer. On rising ground I
have seen jack-rabbits run
straight away from ordinary
greyhounds of native or cold
stock. The greyhounds were
soon willing to quit and
return to camp.
Greyhounds were early introduced on the plains by cattle-
men who had a taste for sport.
Some army officers and
soldiers on the frontier made
a point of bringing out dogs
for the same amusement.
From *The Sporting Dog* by Joseph
A Graham, Macmillan 1904
(Charwynne Dog Features)

Phenotype of American Staghound. can be rough, smoth or wire-haired. (Charwynne Dog Features)

LURCHERS OF THE UNITED STATES

The lurcher function in the United States is mainly carried out there by what is known as Staghounds, big rough-haired cross-bred dogs, cross-bred in pursuit of function not whim, although personal preferences do manifest themselves in conformation. There is an even stronger tradition there too of bobbery packs, a collection of coarsely bred hounds brought together 'to go hunting'. In his *Hunting Dogs* of 1909, (Harding Publishing Co of Columbus, Ohio) Oliver Hartley writes: 'I am a farmer by trade and a racoon hunter for sport, and nothing but a foxhound (a hound used on fox, not our Foxhound, DH) for me, and the better his breeding is the better I like it. I don't care how much noise he makes if he is fast. I like a good tonguer. I only have four hounds at this writing. I have caught 27 'coon and 10 opossum. On the night of November 9th, some friends of mine went out 'coon hunting with me. They had three 'coon dogs and I had four, seven hounds in all. We went about two miles south of where I live to where we sometimes hunt the 'coon.'

In those few words he sums up the global farmer-desire to go hunting with a few functional hounds, in his case 'treeing hounds'. Hartley refers to a Minnesota wolfer who averaged 35 wolves a year and who pinned his faith in the long-eared variety of hounds, with features of strength, endurance, good tonguers and stayers. He had been advised that the best dogs for coyotes are part English blue (Greyhounds, DH) and Russian stag (Borzois, DH). He wrote that the English blue are very fast and the stag are long-winded, with the grit to make a good fight. He wrote that another admired and capable dog is the one-half Scotch stag hound (Scottish Deer-hound, DH) and one-half Greyhound. He recorded that a Wisconsin hunter believed that the best breed to catch and kill coyotes are one-half shepherd (our Collie) and one-half hound, being faster than a hound and trailing just as well on a hot trail. He wrote too that another fast breed for coyotes is a one-fourth English bull, one-fourth Bloodhound and one half Foxhound. Here is a classic example of blending blood in pursuit of performance, the lurcherman's endless quest.

The breed of American Staghound is recognised by their National Kennel Club, with a prescribed breed standard, although it is not recognised by the main American Kennel Club, their equivalent of our KC and principally concerned with show dogs. The American Staghound's standard sets out the need for a hound from 28 to 33 inches in height and from 80 to 100lbs in weight for males, rough-haired, with a hard wiry coat but allowing a long and short-haired variety too. It is described as 'a Greyhound-like breed, built for running but with great power, having been bred for performance for over 100 years, and this shows in its strictly functional conformation… with function never sacrificed for the sake of size.' They are expected to be swift enough to catch coyotes with a head start of more than one-quarter of a mile and powerful enough to bring down the largest of deer. Their need for a long, muscular, arched neck, a deep and wide chest, muscular shoulders with elbows well under and a drawn-up belly is stressed. Commendably, any functional genetic problem is considered 'totally disqualifying'. In Britain, the days when a hound could be stated, in its official description, to be powerful enough to bring down the largest deer have passed.

In his book *The Gun Digest Book of Sporting Dogs*, (DBI Books, Inc, Northbrook, Illinois, 1984), Carl P Wood writes: 'Many other breeds and crossbreeds are used to hunt foxes. Many of these are regional breeds generally used only in one area. They were developed by persons living in that particular area to meet the specific needs of local hunters. These local breeds are not recognised by any official registry, but this does not mean that they are any less efficient or capable at the job for which they were bred. There

COURSING GREYHOUNDS

As in the case of racehorses, Americans have drawn their greyhound blood from the most approved English sources. San Franciso imported quite a number from Australia but the bloodlines were the same, going back to Contango, King Death, and Scotland. Yet, representing from year to year the latest successes in England, the Greentick, Ptarmigan, or Herschel blood came to the fore.

LEFT: **Black-mouthed Cur tree-ing**

BELOW: **'Coon haul.** (Charwynne Dog Features)

are yellow tics, fices, an old breed known as the cur dog, boomers, mountain hounds and many breeds with which I am not at all familiar. In some parts of the country the coursing breeds are used as fox and coyote dogs.' He would have warmed to the lurcher scene in Britain; the concept that hunting dogs, however efficient in the field, are somehow lessened in value by being unrecognised and unregistered, is a seriously flawed one. Pedigree dog breeders in so many countries have closed minds and so often lack experience with sporting dogs in the field.

In his book *Lurchers and Longdogs*, Ted Walsh mentions the Nebraska coyote hound, 29½ inches at the shoulder and weighing 90lb. He quotes from a Minnesota report on the American houndman which states: 'He merely breeds one good hound to another regardless of background... the basis of the American lurcher is the Greyhound crossed first with the Scottish deerhound; secondarily with the Irish Wolfhound and Borzoi; rarely with the whippet or saluki. This breeding pattern may be explained by considering the game coursed in North America, the hare (jack rabbit), red fox and coyote.' This report sets out the use of 'cold blood' or coursing Greyhound on hare, a rougher-coated hound on red fox and the emergence of an American Coyote Hound, 75 to 100lbs, with a Deerhound coat. But it stresses that no kennel there was raising either Deerhounds or Borzois primarily for hunting. The Whippet was recommended for the cotton-tail rabbit, lacking the stamina for the jack-rabbit. In Australia, their lurcher-like running dogs are a type described either as Staghounds, Kangaroo Dogs or Bush Greyhounds. Their similarity illustrates how function dictates form.

An earlier book, *Observations on Borzoi* by Joseph B Thomas (Houghton Mifflin, Boston and New York, 1912), mentions 'turnits', hounds which never run directly after the rabbit, but try to outflank it, taking short-cuts to anticipate its intended course. For this they are disqualified from coursing meetings, yet admired for their guile. Interestingly, Thomas points out that 'the American conditions of hunting are most severe on the hound (he means long-dogs), because he usually has a tremendously long run to overtake this quarry (i.e. coyotes and wolves), who almost invariably has a good head start, and is at best a very swift animal.' He stresses the vital importance of condition in hounds used on coyote and wolf, advising careful feeding, graduated schooling with other skilled animals and a build-up of exercise before hunting.

Thomas considered that puppy-schooling was vital for coursing dogs, with early and gradual conditioning essential, giving the view that 'I do not believe that any hound that has not worked in puppyhood can possibly acquire, after he has reached the age of one or two years, sufficient staying power and love of the game ever to become really good.' It is worth noting his stressing both stamina and keenness to hunt. He emphasised the importance of matching breeding, training, condition and experience in the making of a good coyote or wolf dog. He wrote: 'There are not many hounds of any breed that will tackle a coyote or wolf without proper training; and without experience, it can be said that it is impossible for any hound even to catch a coyote. Most Western wolf-hunters have packs of hounds, picked up here and there, that are kept merely because of their performances, regardless of their breeding, shape or color'. Sounds like a sensible lurcherman!

He concluded by writing: 'These hounds, which run loose all year, traveling at times sixty to seventy miles a day, are of all sorts of coursing blood, greyhound, deerhound, and Borzoi. The conditions of coursing wolves or coyotes are most difficult. In places the country is very rough, and the coyote generally gets a long start, sometimes more than half a mile. He is surprisingly swift, so that it takes a good hound to catch him. He is also a surprisingly good fighter, so that it is asking a good deal of any animal in coming, winded, upon a coyote to tackle it'. The ancestors of these dogs would have undertaken the long journey to a new life in America, nearly always from the British Isles; the function of the lurcher was merely transported across the Atlantic. For hunters, America is still the place to be for freedom to continue the sporting pastimes of your ancestors. We have all but lost that freedom.

Maggie the 'roo dog. (from the famous Wheatbelt line)

SOUTH AUSTRALIAN STAGHOUND
Sire: from line of Irish Wolfhound – Deerhound – Greyhound crosses.
Dam: Deerhound x Greyhound.

KANGAROO HOUNDS IN AUSTRALIA

For some time, by a succession of enormous bounds, the animal keeps far ahead of his pursuers – especially when running uphill, where he is as much favoured by his long hindlegs, as a hare is by hers, and all are soon lost to the sight of unmounted hunters. When he has been overtaken and brought to bay, one of the trained dogs keeps him there; and this he does barking round and round him, threatening every moment to fly at him. The other dog returns to the hunters, and leads them to the spot where his companion is detaining the kangaroo; and so completely does the noisy assailant engage the attention of the unfortunate beast, that the hunters are frequently enabled to approach unperceived, and stun him with a blow over the head. An old kangaroo is there termed by the hunters 'an old man' the flesh of a young one is, however, by many considered very delicate eating. A powerful dog will kill a small kangaroo single-handed; and if properly taught will then seek for his master, and conduct him to the body.

From *Dog Breaking* Hutchinson, 1909
(Charwynne Dog Features)

AUSTRALIAN LURCHERS

Australian Lurcher.
Sire: ¾ Wolfhound, ¼ Greyhound.
Dam: Deerhound x Greyhound.

Australian Staghound.

KANGAROO LURCHERS

'Some say they were a blend of Scotch Collie and Greyhound, others Greyhound, Collie and Mastiff, and so on. The truth is they were made by crossing the Deer (not Stag) Hound and Greyhound with a little Cattle-dog as well. The first dogs were very big, bony devils, with a light coat of shaggy hair; game as Bulldogs and fierce as tiger-cats. They ran both by scent and sight; some, but not many, of the present dogs do the same. One of them was a match for any kangaroo or dingo that ever walked.'

Robert Kaleski, Endeavour Press, *Australian Barkers and Biters*, Sydney, 1914

BUSH GREYHOUNDS

'All round the old settled districts where the hares are you will find Greyhounds. Not the slim, race-horse-looking ones of the coursing ground, but bigger, rougher and bonier – more like the Kangaroo-dog. The reason of the difference is very simple. The game, when hunted, has a number of cowardly tricks, such as doubling short round stumps and logs, running amongst rocks and gravel patches, or through mud and tussocks. This wears the coursing Greyhound out very quickly, not being what he has a right to expect; so to be any good he is crossed with the Kangaroo-dog and the progeny are Bush Greyhounds.'

Robert Kaleski, Endeavour Press, *Australian Barkers and Biters*, Sydney, 1914

Hunters Going Out In The Morning by Samual Howitt, from an original drawing by Captain T Williamson. Courtesy of Hobhouse Ltd. (Charwynne Dog Features)

LEFT: **Sighthounds are prized all over the Middle East, North and Northern-Central Africa.**
Arnout of Cairo by Jean Leon Gerome (1824–1904)

BELOW: **Coursing Greyhounds: redundant skills.**
(Charwynne Dog Features)

CONCLUSION

KEEPING THE FAITH

'I have tried Greyhounds but they are no good in rough country, too easily hurt. Deerhounds are the tops; gave up Borzois after five years, too temperamental (like the Russians). Wolfhounds can be very game but are not fast enough. Afghans are a write-off, too much coat and no brains. Salukis are a lovely hound, fast and tough but they are the only breed of dog I could not control, could not get 'through' to them.'

Those words from an experienced Australian hunter of 'roos, emus, feral pig and foxes, of nearly fifty years ago are worth heeding. But they apply to his terrain, his quarry and his climate; lurchermen here know that they need a different dog on different quarry, although the dreaded hunting ban has limited the latter. Who now, for legally taken quarry, needs a lurcher over 24 inches at the withers? Who now needs a dog capable of bringing down the bigger quarry?

Will we ever again need the type of instinctive hunting technique described by Sobieski in his *Lays of the Deer Forest* of 1848, when he wrote: 'The experienced greyhounds rarely run at the deer's neck but come up close by his flank, and shoot up at his throat, too close for the blow of his horns, and to effect this they will sometimes for several yards run by his haunch until the favourable moment for making this launch at his neck. There are, however, dogs which have peculiar modes of attack. Thus some will seize the deer by the fetlock, and one hound named Factor, a small but very fleet and highly couraged dog, was accustomed to make a spring over the deer's croup and fix himself upon the nape of his neck, when he never failed to bring him down.'

There is a dilemma here for the 'bleeding hearts brigade'; which gives the greater potential suffering on a deer cull, the possibility of maiming from long range or the certainty of seizing at close range? Animal welfare sadly is so often much more linked with a prejudice against hunting than truly and honestly about reducing animal suffering. Academics who don't approve of hunting don't always approve of truth and accuracy either. I recently read a thick tome on post-medieval Germany and was alarmed to discover that not only was hunting not mentioned in the index but didn't feature in the text! The book covered a period of German history when their leaders went hunting six days out of seven! Did that have absolutely no impact on who they entertained, who they spoke to on a daily basis, how decisions were reached, how social life developed? Selective scholarship deceives, perhaps knowingly.

Which feature is of the greater value to the reduction of suffering in animals that have to be controlled, the Foxhound which can kill a fox with one bite or a so-called 'marksman' who can maim at long distance? Which pig being driven to the slaughter house suffers more, one urged on by a cattle-probe or one driven by dogs? Which harms African wild hoofed-game more, being chased by a low-flying helicopter, darted with drugs and then tagged or, being 'seized' by a strapping hunting dog and then tagged? The broad-mouthed 'holding' dogs can seize and hold quarry and not leave a mark on it. Soon blind prejudice not knowledge or prowess will triumph and we will lose hunting dogs with irreplaceable skills. There is sense surely in retaining their blood, keeping the lines going, as the saying goes.

In his book *Hunters All* (Huddlesford, 1986), Brian Plummer describes Phil Lloyd's way of catching deer: 'Lloyd perfected his own technique of deer poaching allowing his dog a hock hold and nothing more, training his dogs by allowing them to 'bulldog' Hereford calves until they had developed the technique of pinning a deer without damaging it, so that Phil could despatch the beast quickly, quietly and above all, humanely.' The act was illegal but the skill displayed by the dog was remarkable and a skill surely of value today in wildlife conservation work, when tagging or emergency treatment is deemed necessary. Most dogs want to work, it is the human intent which directs that urge to beneficial purposes. Dogs which earn their keep are always better valued.

In the early nineteenth century, William Scrope had the freedom of the Atholl deer forest, to kill the venison needed for the castle, to run the drives for the castle's guests and to conduct culls when needed. Unable to obtain efficient pure Deerhounds, he resorted to a cross between the Foxhound and the greyhound, with great success. Scrope recorded that the head stalker, a Mr John Crerar, had tried various crosses over sixty years, but found this mix incomparably the best. Scrope wrote that 'the Greyhound cannot stand the weather, and wants courage... and they have no nose... The Foxhound is equally objectionable; he has not sufficient speed, gives tongue and hunts too much by scent; in this way he spreads alarm through the forest.' But he stressed the need to re-breed the hybrids *not* to 'continue to breed from the produce first obtained'. That is an interesting point for lurcher breeders seeking to capitalise on proven stock.

In her absorbing book, *The Grunter Hunters* (Halcyon Press, 1992), Kim Swan describes how feral pig is controlled in New Zealand using brave and determined dogs. The boar she hunts can weigh over 250lb and frequently kill hunting dogs. She and her fellow hunters use boar-lurchers: Bull Terrier and Bullmastiff crosses, Rottweiler blood and a regular infusion of cattle dog blood too. Feral pig do enormous damage to farmland in New Zealand, they are not native species, but are descended from domestic pigs which have escaped, gone wild and interbred, perhaps from 14 different types or breeds of domestic pig. The dogs have to be immensely courageous, extraordinarily agile, extremely resolute and supremely athletic – or they die! When the wild boar population here needs culling, it would be best done using seizing dogs, that is, if we haven't destroyed all those with strong heads and displaying 'persistence', as the police and RSPCA like to term it!

Currently, the lurcher which best earns its keep is probably the rabbit-dog working to the lamp. The great George Smith has written on this subject: 'As regards the breeding of lurchers for lamping this, like so much to do with lurchers, is a matter of opinion. But the best lamping dogs I have ever had were "Lass", who carried Staffordshire bull terrier, Whippet and greyhound blood; "Spring", a Bedlington–greyhound; "Fin", who looked Deerhound–greyhound but had everything else besides, and stood nearly 30 inches at the shoulder; and one pure greyhound. As I have said, many people favour the small greyhound–Collie for lamping but the truth is that the really good dog will do his work, no matter what he looks like.' Whatever its use, the 'really good dog' will always triumph, whatever its size; keeping that blood alive is of paramount importance. May today's lurcher-men honour the work of those who went before them, triumph over what Laurence Van Der Post has described as 'town thinking' and perpetuate these remarkable hunting dogs for future hunters.

'This is the very race of dogs applicable to the aggregate wants of the poacher... no other breed of the whole species seems so peculiarly calculated for the purpose. They equal, if they do not excell, any other dog in sagacity, and are easily taught any thing that is possible for an animal of this description to acquire by instruction. Some of the best lurchers are but little inferior in speed to many well-formed Greyhounds; rabbits they kill to a certainty.'

William Taplin, *The Sportsman's Cabinet*, 1803

'It is time for all sportsmen to unite to maintain their sports in being. Strange though it may seem to them, it is even time for the anti-field sports organisations to realise that they can no longer regard field sportsmen as their opponents. Every field sports enthusiast is keen to see the larks hovering in the sky above him and to hear the birds continuing to sing in the hedgerows... it is the hunter's natural if contradictory impulse to preserve what he hunts.'

Michael Brander, *The Hunting Instinct*, Oliver & Boyd, 1964

Australian Wheatbelt Staghound. Saluki blood was added to improve heat tolerance.

Dinha the lurcher at work.

Sloughis.

Whippet blood valued in lurchers.
A Lurcher, Malcolm Coward, 20th Century

GLOSSARY OF TERMS

angulation – the degree of slope or angle of the shoulder-blade in the forequarters and in the sharp angles of the inter-related bones in the hindquarters – thigh, hock and metatarsus.

barrel-hocks (spread hocks) – hocks turning out resulting in feet with inward-pointing toes (similar to bandy legs).

barrel-ribbed – well rounded rib cage.

belton – a colour designation in which white and coloured hair intermingles (blue belton, liver belton, orange belton etc.).

bird dog – a sporting dog specialising in the hunting of birds.

blanket – the coat-colour on the back from the withers to the rump.

blaze – a white strip of hair in the centre of the face usually between the eyes.

bloom – the sheen of a coat in prime condition.

bodied up – well developed in maturity.

button ear – the ear flap folding forward usually towards the eye.

cat-feet – the rounded short-toed foot effect.

chiselled – clean cut particularly in the head.

chopping – as for paddling but exaggerated forward rather than out to the side.

close-coupled – comparatively short from withers to hip bones.

cobby – short-bodied, compact in torso.

coupled – hindquarters connected to torso.

cow-hocks – hocks turned toward each other (similar to knock-knees).

dewlaps – loose, pendulous skin under the throat.

dish-faced – concavity in the nasal bone making the nose higher at the tip than the stop.

drive – a solid thrust from the hindquarters, denoting sound locomotion.

drop ears – the ends of the ear folded or drooping forward.

dudley nose – flesh-coloured or brown-nosed

elbows out – the positioning of the elbow away from the body.

even bite – meeting of both sets of front teeth at edges with no overlap.

feathering – distinctly longer hair on rear line of legs, back of ears and underside of tail.

flecking – coat markings from groups of different coloured hairs.

flews – upper lips pendulous, particularly at their inner corners.

gay tail – the tail carried up on high (usually used when carried so incorrectly for the breed).

grizzle – bluish-grey or steel-grey in colour of coat.

hackney-gait (or-action) – high stepping motion of the front legs.

hare-feet – a foot whose third digits are longer, an elongated foot.

haw – membrane in the inside corner of the eye, usually reddy pink.

layback
(used loosely) – the angle of the shoulder as compared with the vertical.
(or strictly) – an undershot jaw with a receding nose.

lay of shoulder – angled position of the shoulder.

leather – the flap of the ear.

level bite (pincer bite) – when the front teeth of both the jaws meet exactly.

linty – firm twisty condition of coat, with plenty of spring in it.

lumber – superfluous flesh.

mask – dark shading on the foreface.

merle – blue-grey flecked with black, in colour of coat.

occipital crest – peak of upper rear point of skull.

out at elbow – see elbows out.

overshot jaw – the upper jaw's front teeth overlapping (pig-jawed in excess).

overspring ribs – exaggerated curvature of ribcage.

paddling – a heavy clumsy threshing action of the forelegs in which the feet swing wide of the body when on the move.

pile – dense undercoat of soft hair.

pily – a coat of mixed soft woolly and long wiry hair.

pincer-bite – see level bite.

plaiting (or weaving or crossing) – the movement of one front leg across the path of the other front leg in the dog's gait.

prick-ear – carried erect and usually pointed at the tip.

ribbed up – long last rib.

roach-backed (carp-backed) – with a convex curved back towards the loin

roan – a fine equal mixture of coloured and white hairs (blue roan etc.).

rose ear – a small drop ear which folds over and back.

saddle-backed – with a soft or sagging back (from weak muscles or over-long back).

scissors bite – in which the outer side of the lower incisors touches the inner side of the upper incisors.

set on – join (of say tail root to torso).

short-coupled – see close-coupled.

shoulder lay-back – see layback.

snipiness – condition in which the muzzle is too pointed, weak-looking.

splay-feet – flat, open-toed, over-spread feet.

stop – indentation where the nasal bone meets the skull between the eyes.

straight shoulders – straight up and down shoulder blades, lacking correct angulation.

sway-back – concave curvature of the back line between the withers and the hip bones.

tail carried gaily – see gay tail.

throatiness – an excess of loose skin under the throat.

ticked – small isolated areas of black or coloured hairs on white.

topknot – a tuft of longer hair on the top and front of the head.

topline – the dog's outline from just behind the withers to the rump.

undershot jaw – the malformation of the jaw which projects the lower jaw and incisors beyond the upper (a sign of this in small puppies is that they appear to be grinning).

well angulated – good sharp angle in the thigh–hock–metatarsus area.

well-coupled – well made in the area from the withers to the hip-bones.

well-knit – neat and compactly constructed and connected.

well-laid – soundly placed and correctly angled.

well laid back (shoulders) – oblique shoulders ideally slanting at 45° to the ground.

well let-down – close to the ground, having short hocks.

well ribbed up – ribs neither too long nor too wide apart; compact.

well-sprung – with well-rounded ribs.

well tucked-up – excessively small waist; absence of visible abdomen from the side-view (as in Greyhounds).

yawing (crabbing) – movement with the body travelling in a line at an angle with the line of movement of the legs.

THE ANATOMY OF THE DOG

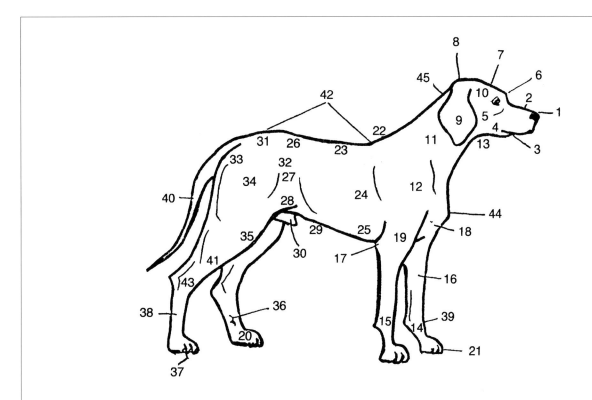

1.	Nose	24.	Ribs
2.	Muzzle	25.	Chest
3.	Lips	26.	Loin
4.	Flews	27.	Flank
5.	Cheek	28.	Groin
6.	Stop	29.	Belly or Abdomen
7.	Foretace	30.	Sheath
8.	Peak or Occiput	31.	Croup
9.	Ear	32.	Hip
10.	Brow	33.	Rump
11.	Neck	34.	Thigh (Upper) (First)
12.	Shoulder	35.	Stifle or Knee
13.	Dewlap	36.	Dewclaw
14.	Pastern or Metacarpus	37.	Toenail
15.	Wrist or Carpus	38.	Metatarsus or Hind Pastern
16.	Forearm	39.	Knee or Manus
17.	Elbow	40.	Tail or Stern
18.	Brisket	41.	Thigh (Lower) (Second)
19.	Upper Arm	42.	Topline
20.	Foot	43.	Hock
21.	Toes or Digits	44.	Sternum or Breast Bone
22.	Withers	45.	Crest
23.	Back		

Strongly built coarsely bred hounds span the centuries.
Floor tile decorated with the Gonzaga impresa (emblem) a white hound *c.*1492–94.
Workshop of Antonio dei Fedeli (attrib).
(Charwynne Dog Features)

BIBLIOGRAPHY

Blood Sport, Hunting in Britain since 1066 Emma Griffin, Yale, 2007

Dogs in Antiquity, Anubis to Cerberus Douglas Brewer, Terence Clark and Adrian Phillips, 2001

Hunters All, Brian Plummer, Huddlesford, 1986

I Walked By Night, edited by L Rider Haggard, Nicholson & Watson, 1935

Lurchers and Longdogs, E G Walsh, Standfast, 1977

Medieval Hunting, Richard Almond, Sutton, 2003

Observations on Borzoi, Joseph B Thomas, Houghton Miflin, 1912

On Hunting, (Al-Mansur's book) compiled by Sir Terence Clark and Muawiya Derhalli, Aris & Phillips Ltd., 2001

On Hunting with Hounds, Xenophon & Arrian, edited by A A Phillips & M M Willcock, 1999

Swifter than the Arrow, the Golden Hunting Hounds of Ancient Egypt Michael Rice, Tauris, 2006

The Complete Book of Sight Hounds, Long Dogs and Lurchers, Brian Plummer, Robinson, 1991

The Confessions of a Poacher, J Connell, 1901, reprinted as *The King of the Poachers* by Tideline, 1983

The Dog in Sport, James Wentworth Day, Harrap, 1938

The Greyhound, H Edwards Clarke, Popular Dogs, 1965

The Hawk and the Hound, The Art of Medieval Hunting John Cummins, Weidenfeld & Nicolson, 1988

The Hunting Instinct, Michael Brander, Oliver & Boyd, 1964

The Whippet Handbook, W Lewis Renwick, Nicholson & Watson, 1957

INDEX